GARDEN

COLORING BOOK

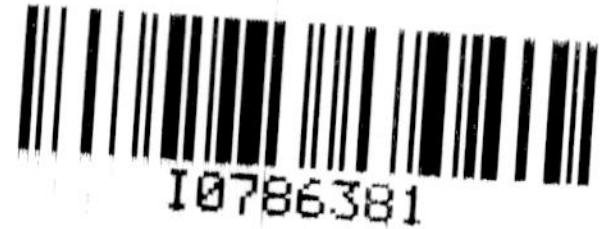

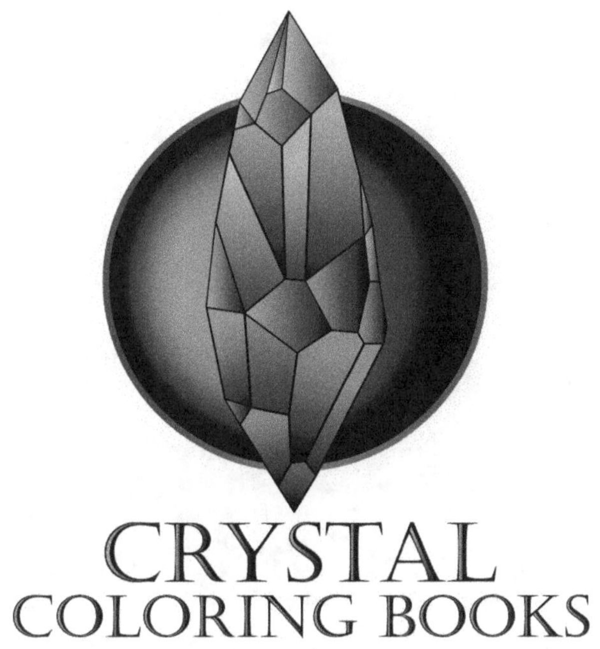

CRYSTAL
COLORING BOOKS

ISBN-13: 978-1725876750
ISBN-10: 1725876752

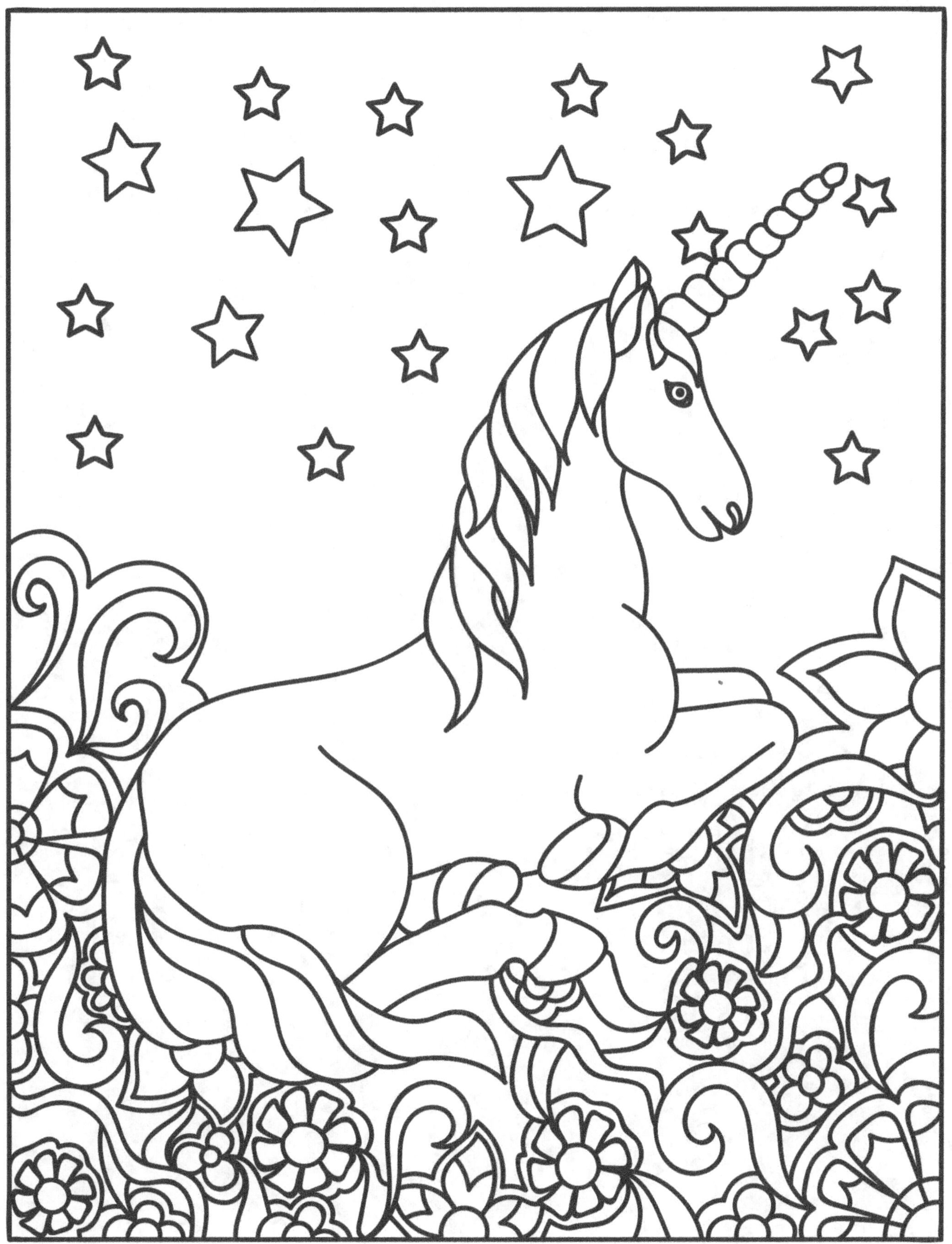

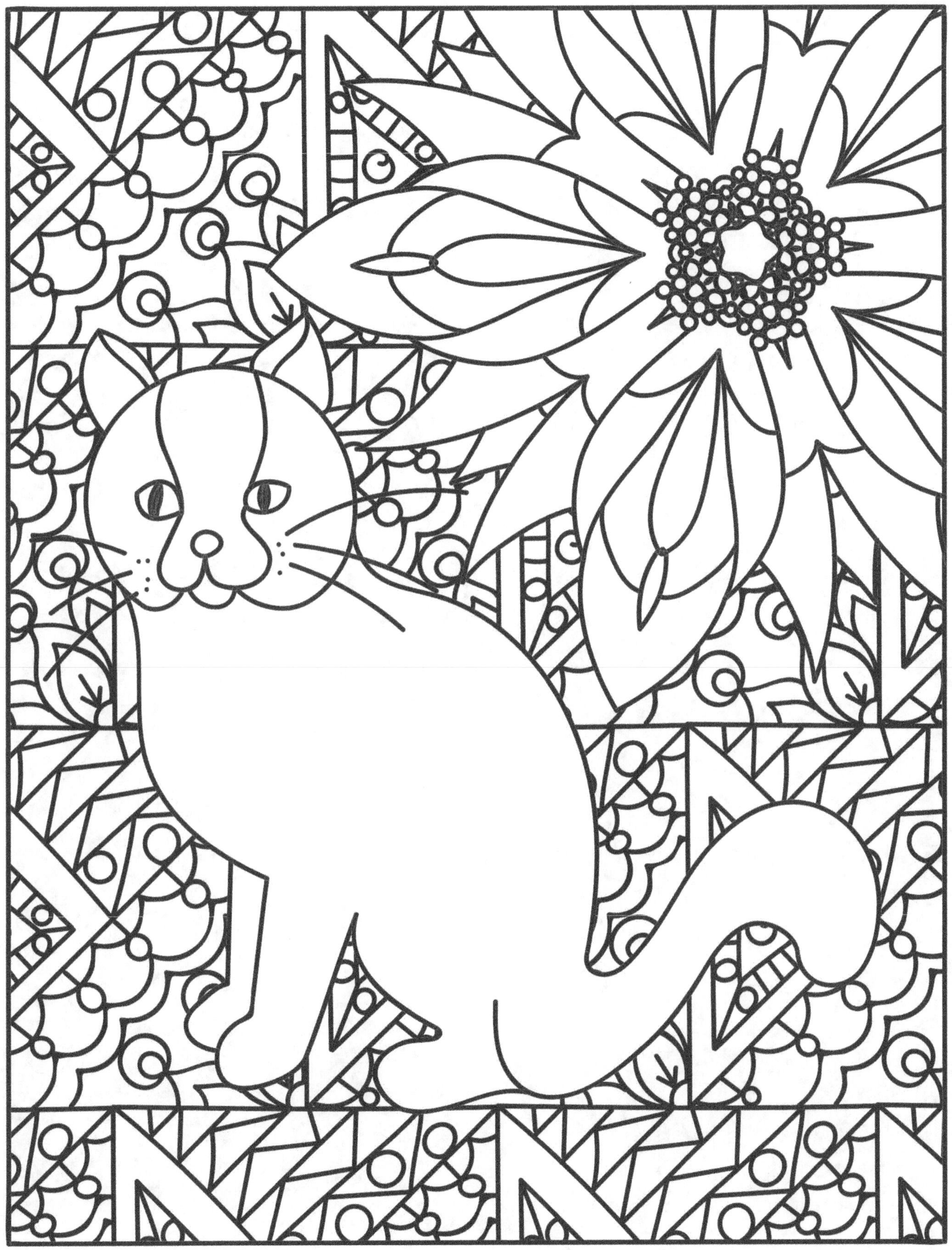

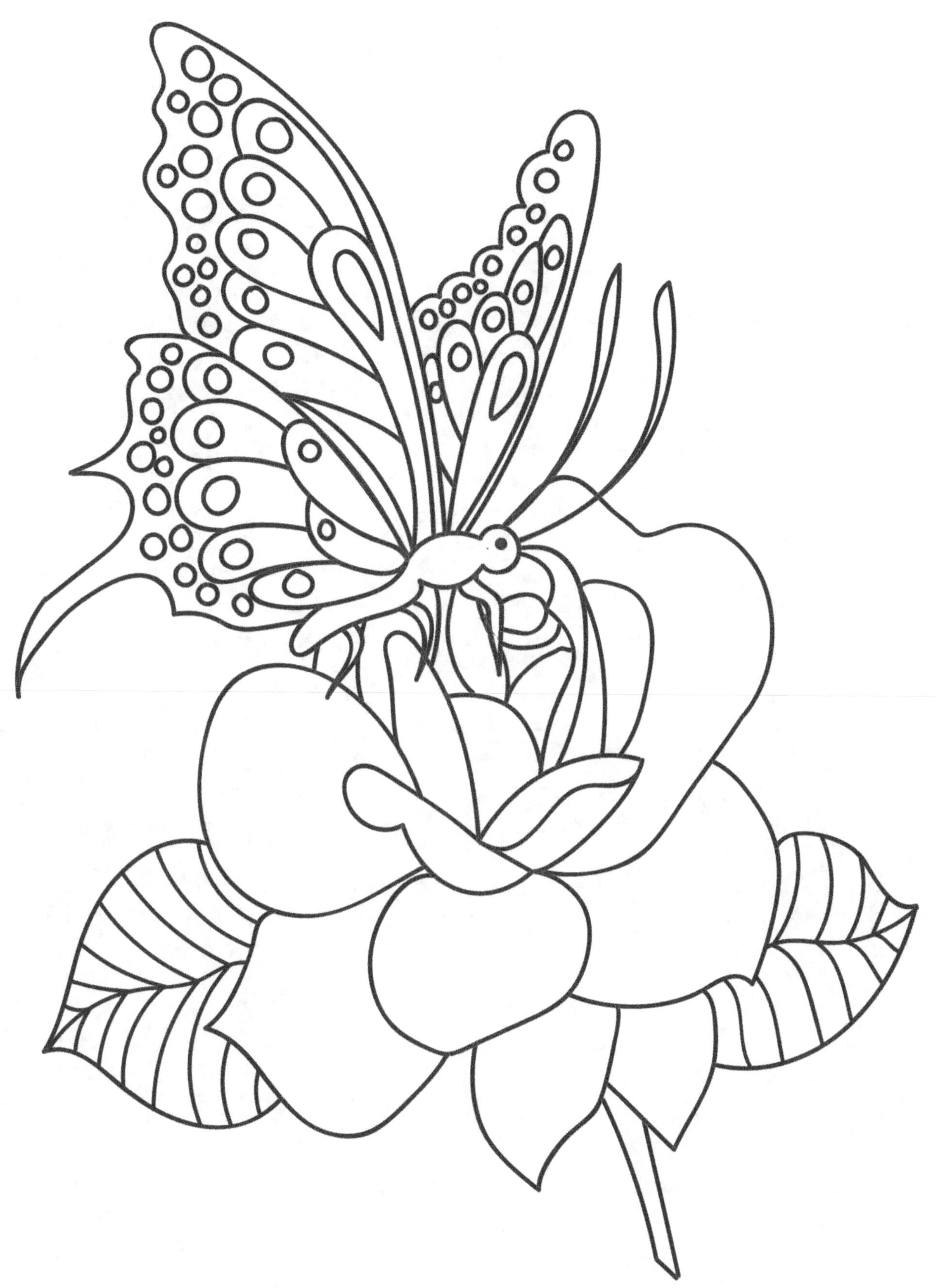

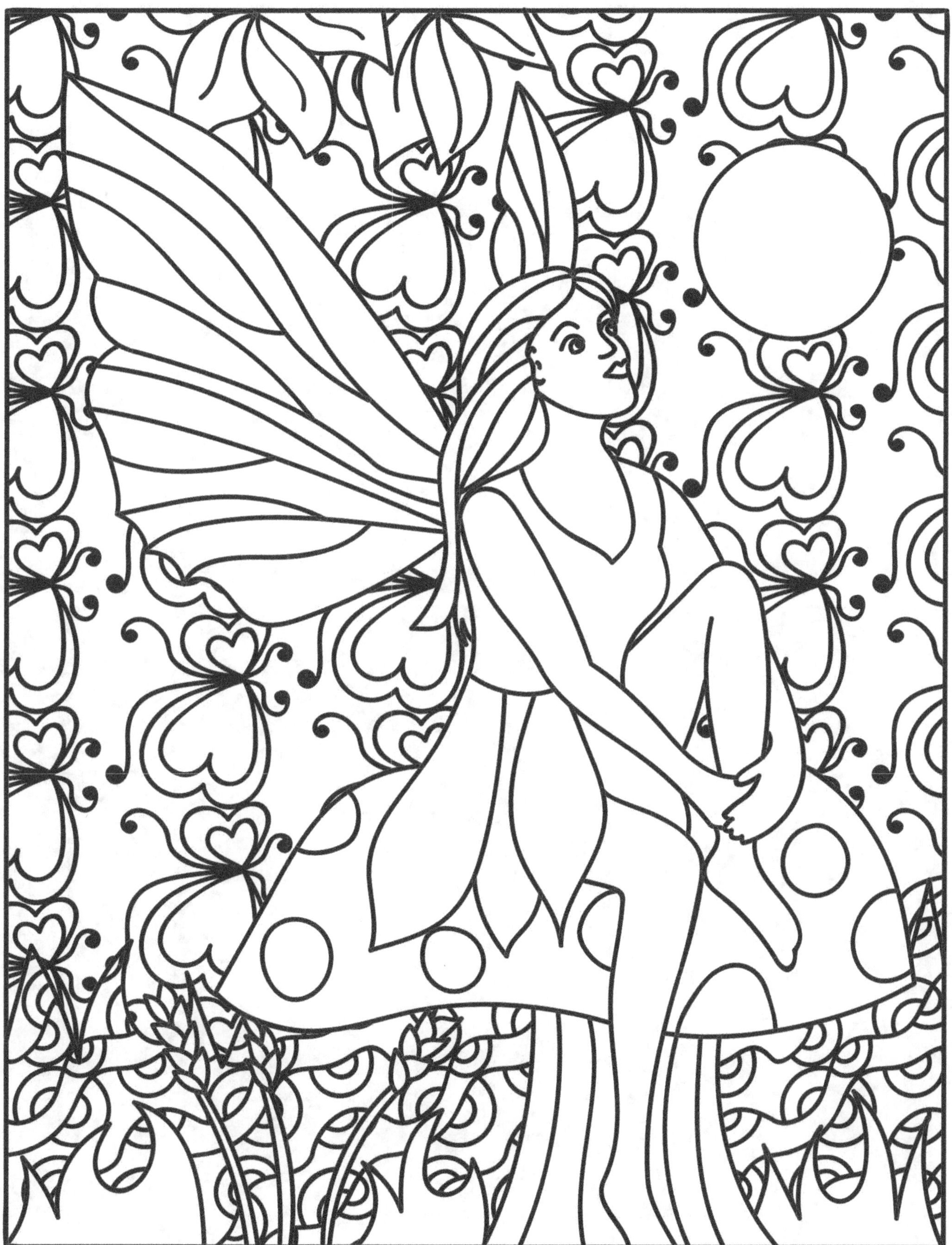

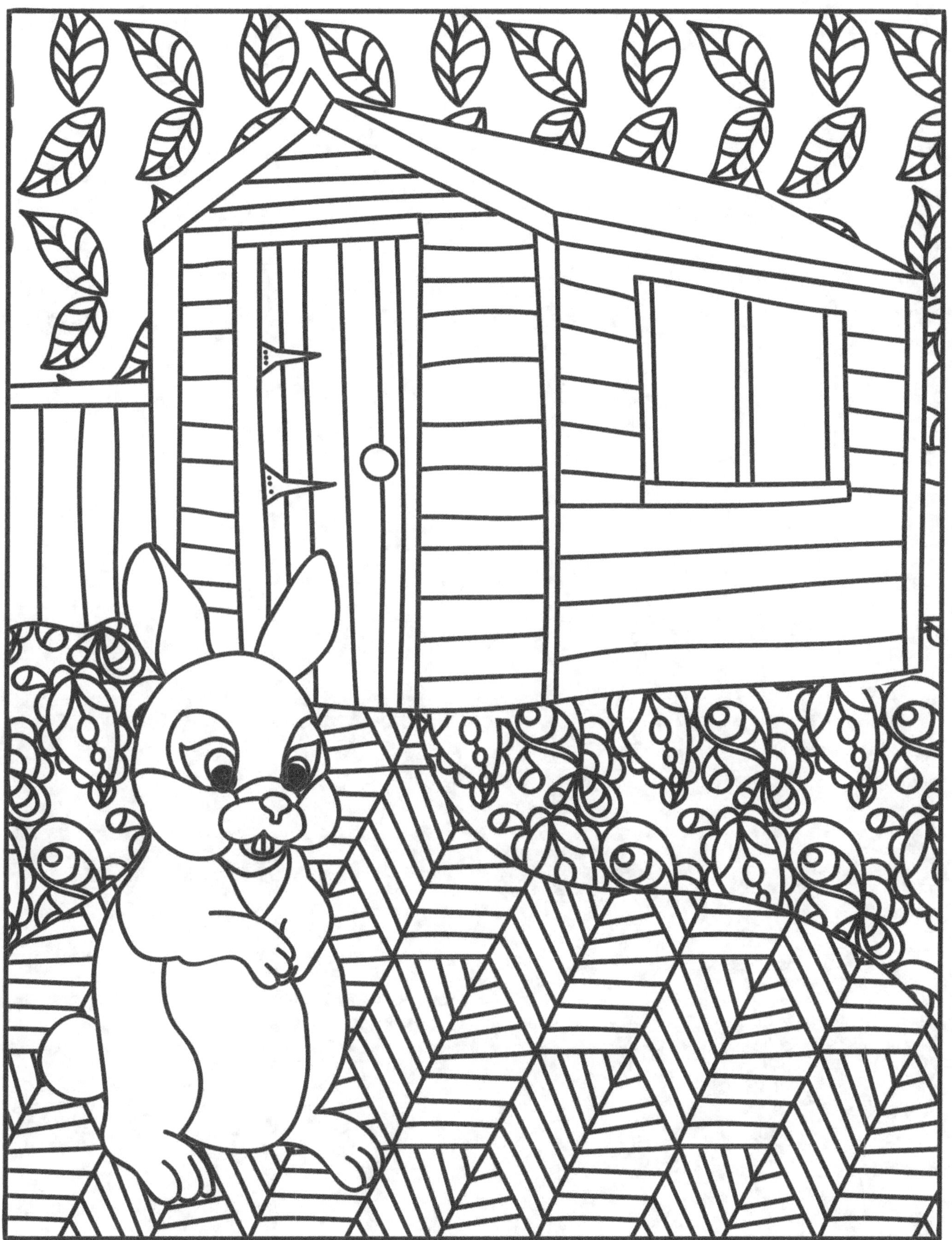

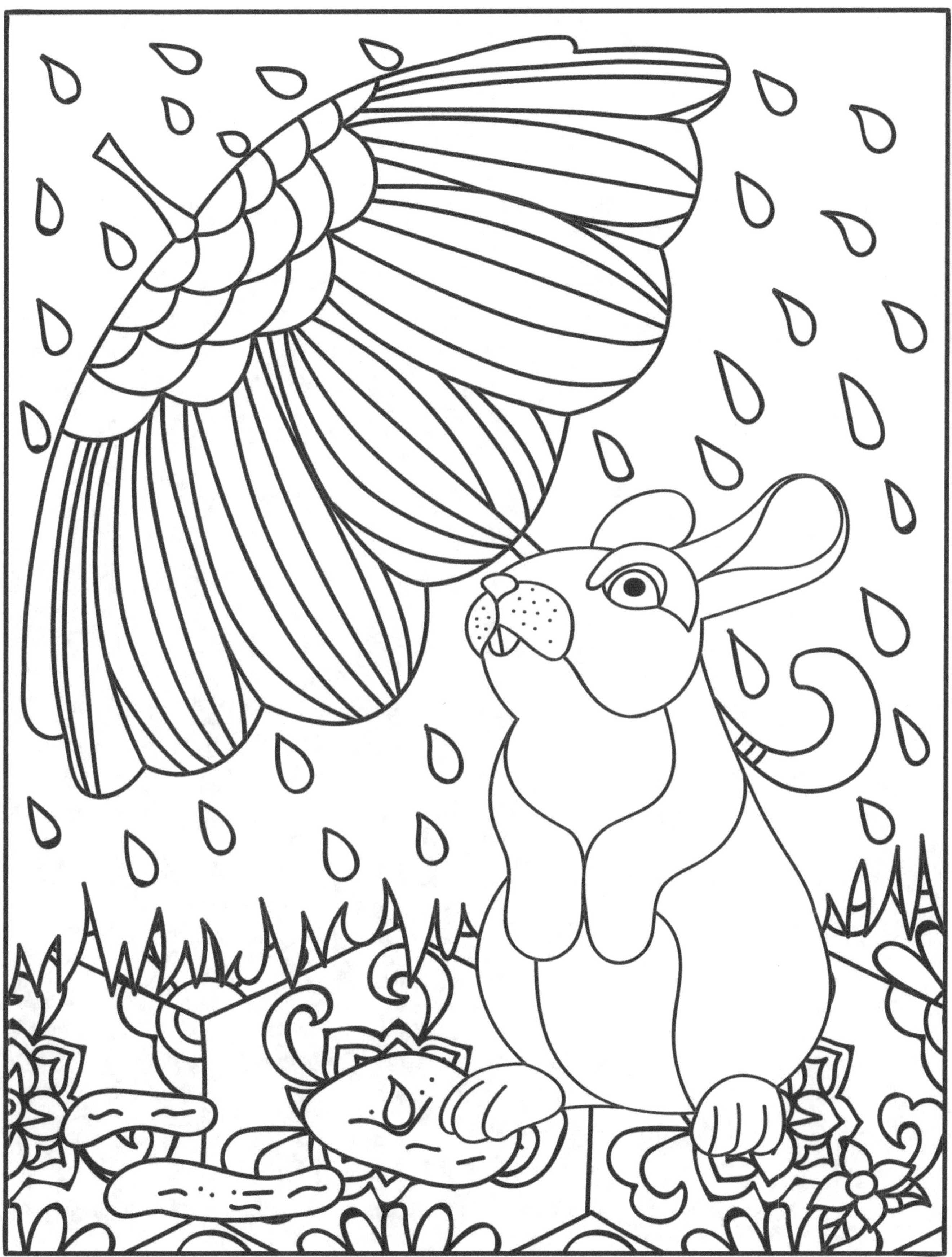

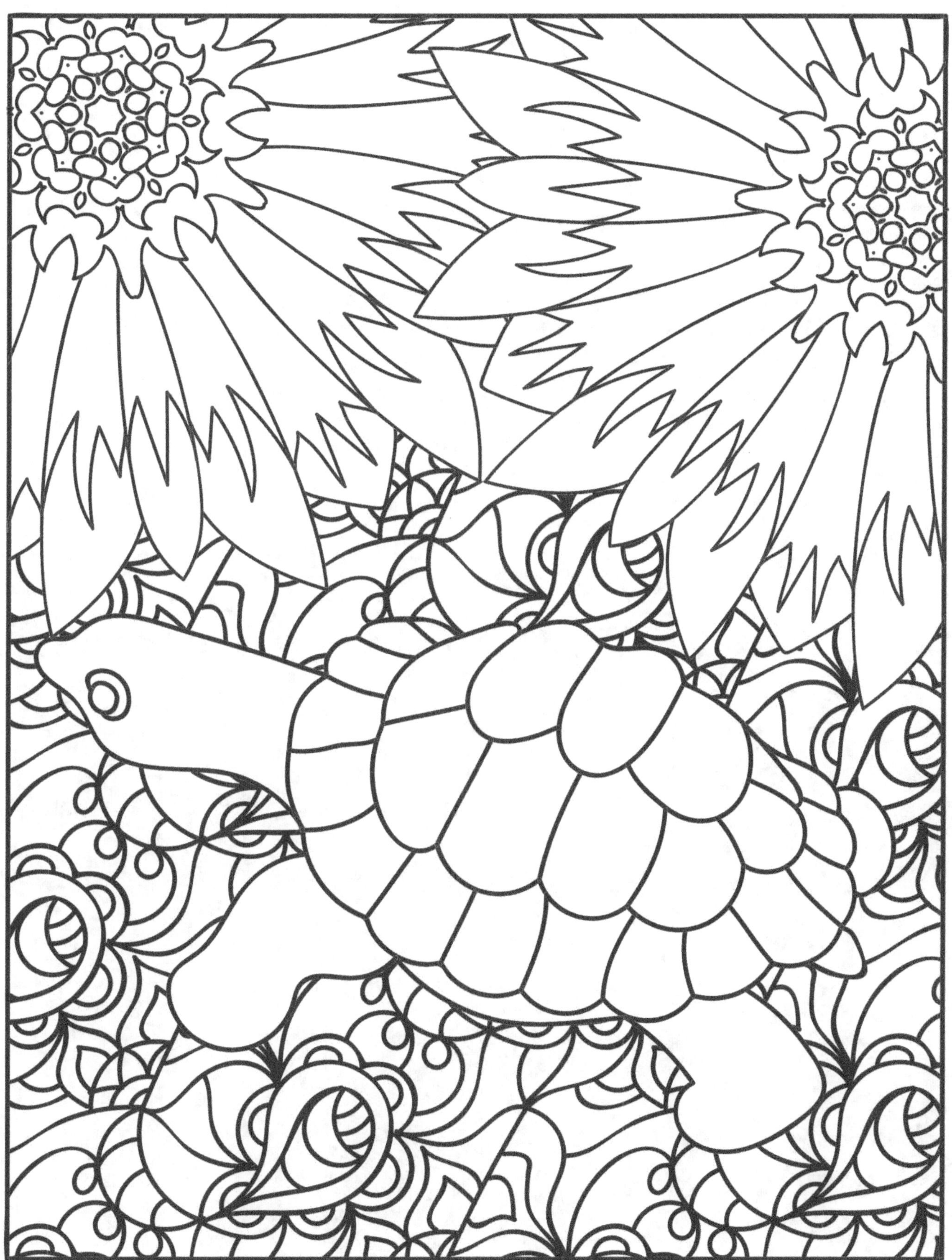

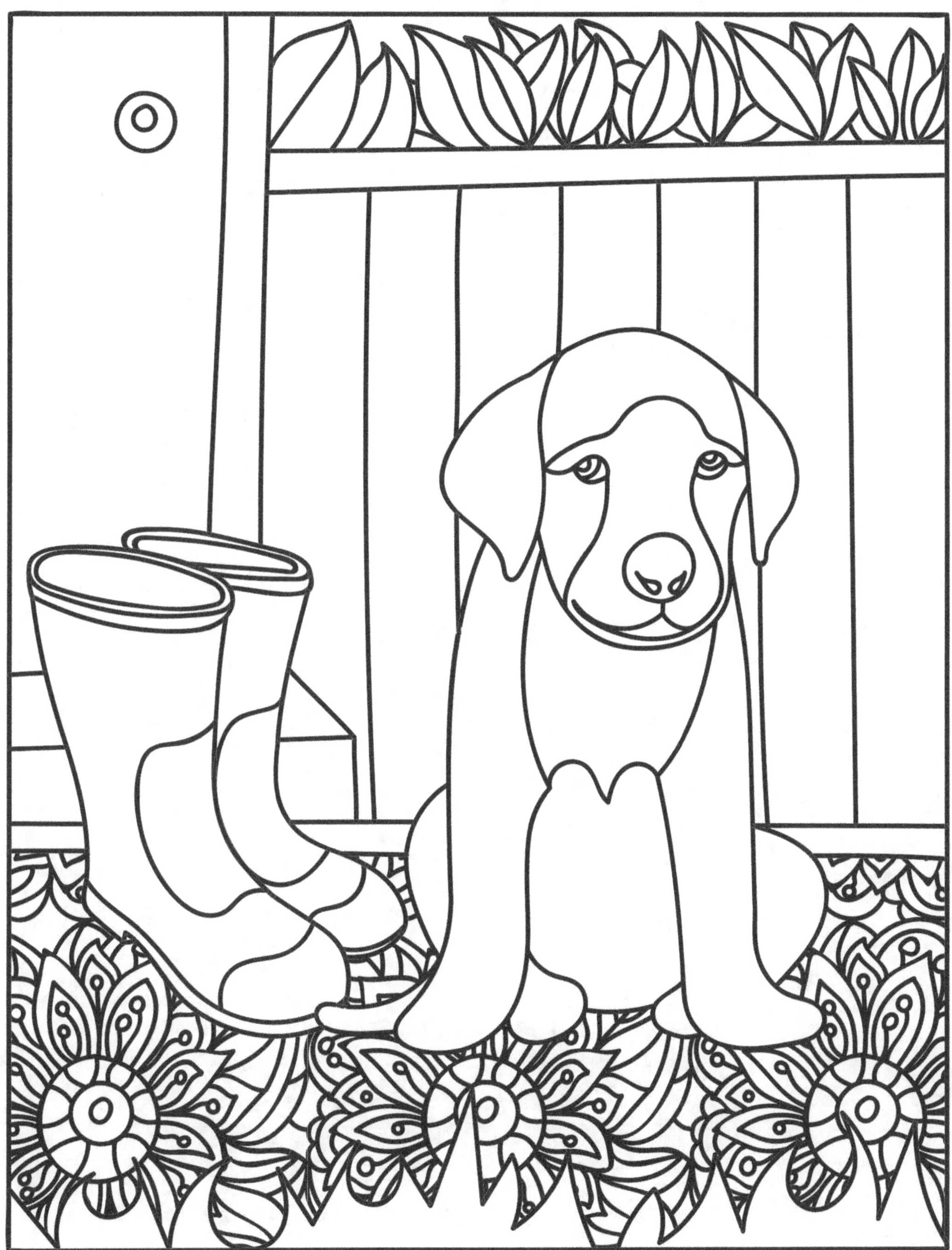

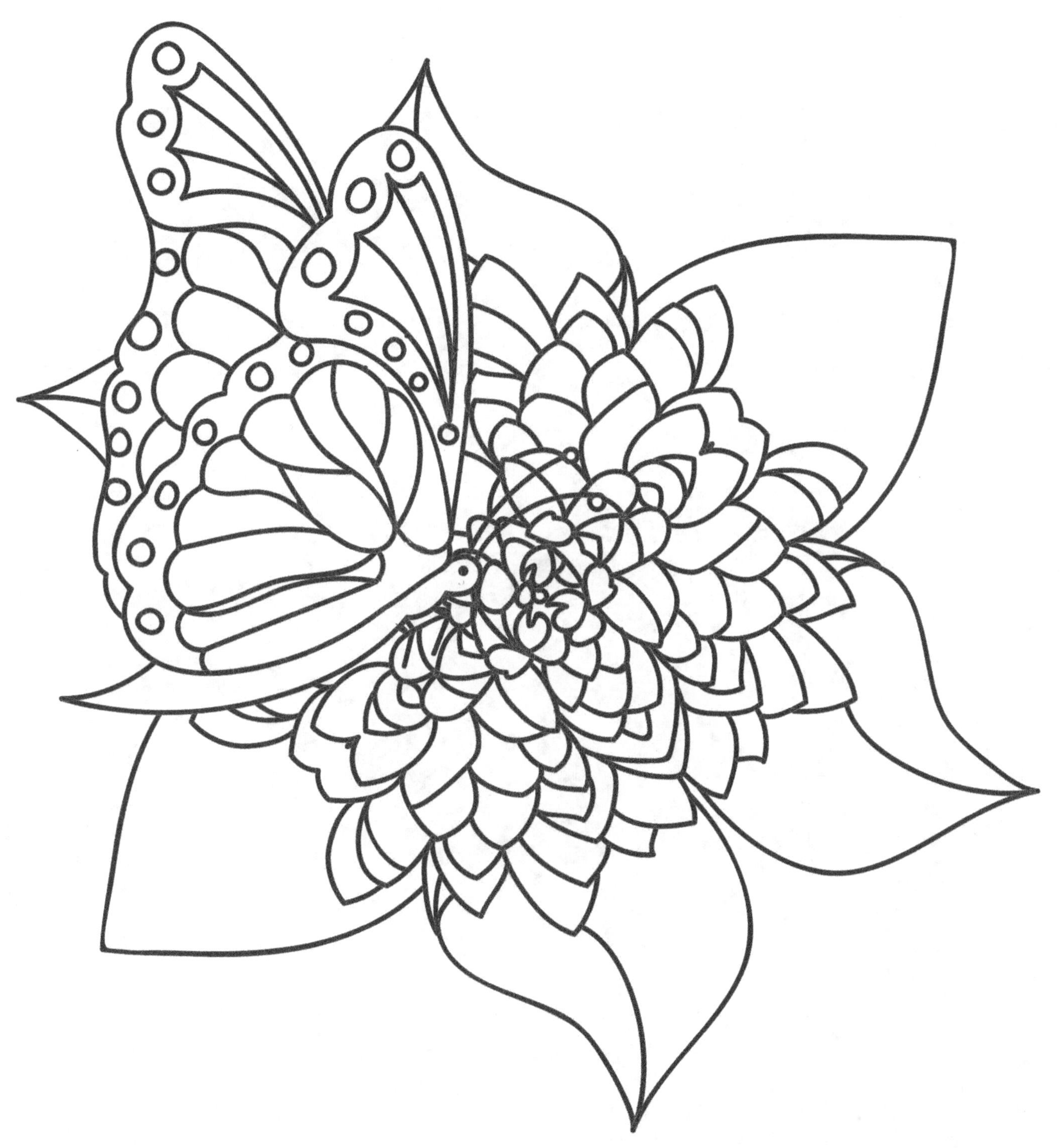

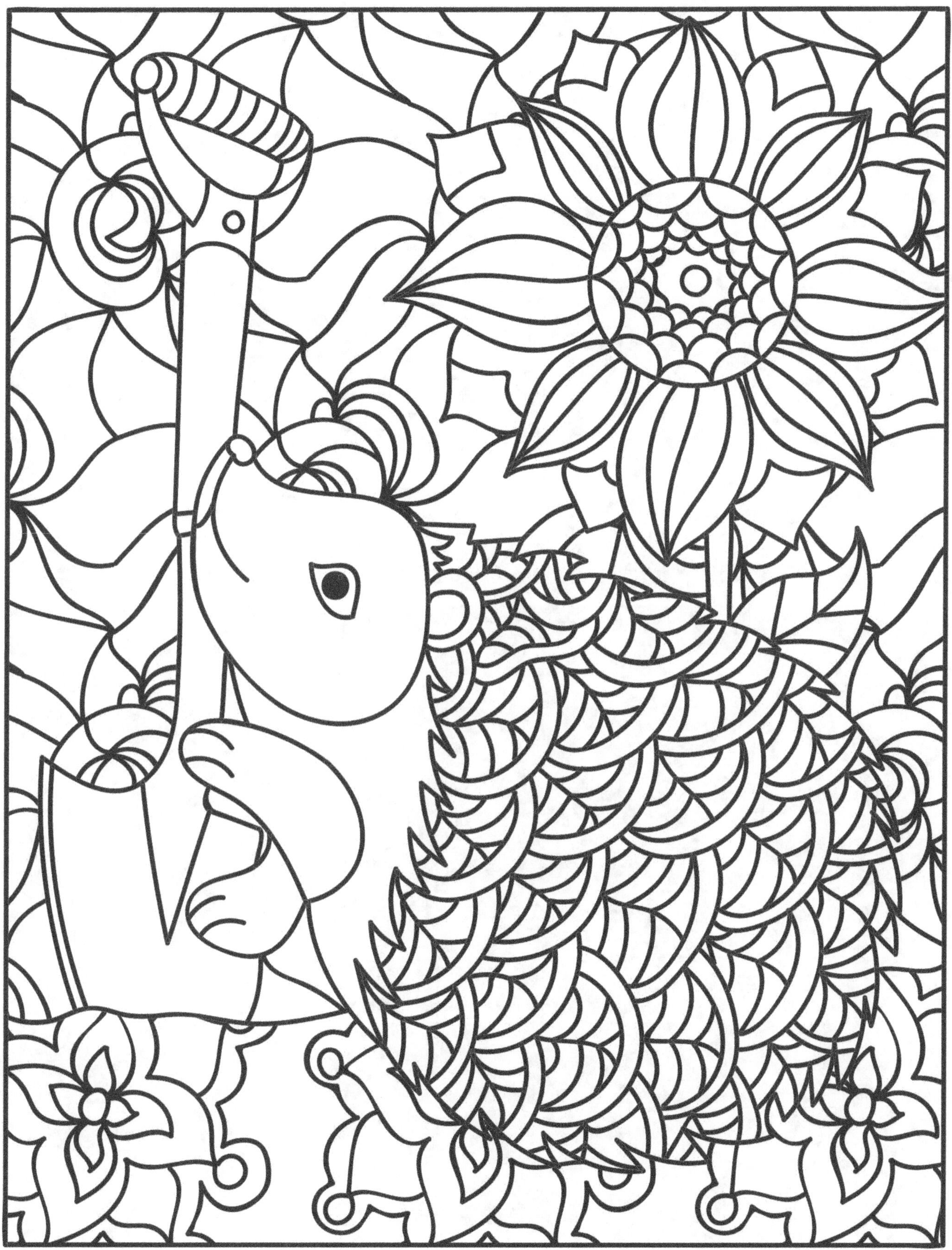

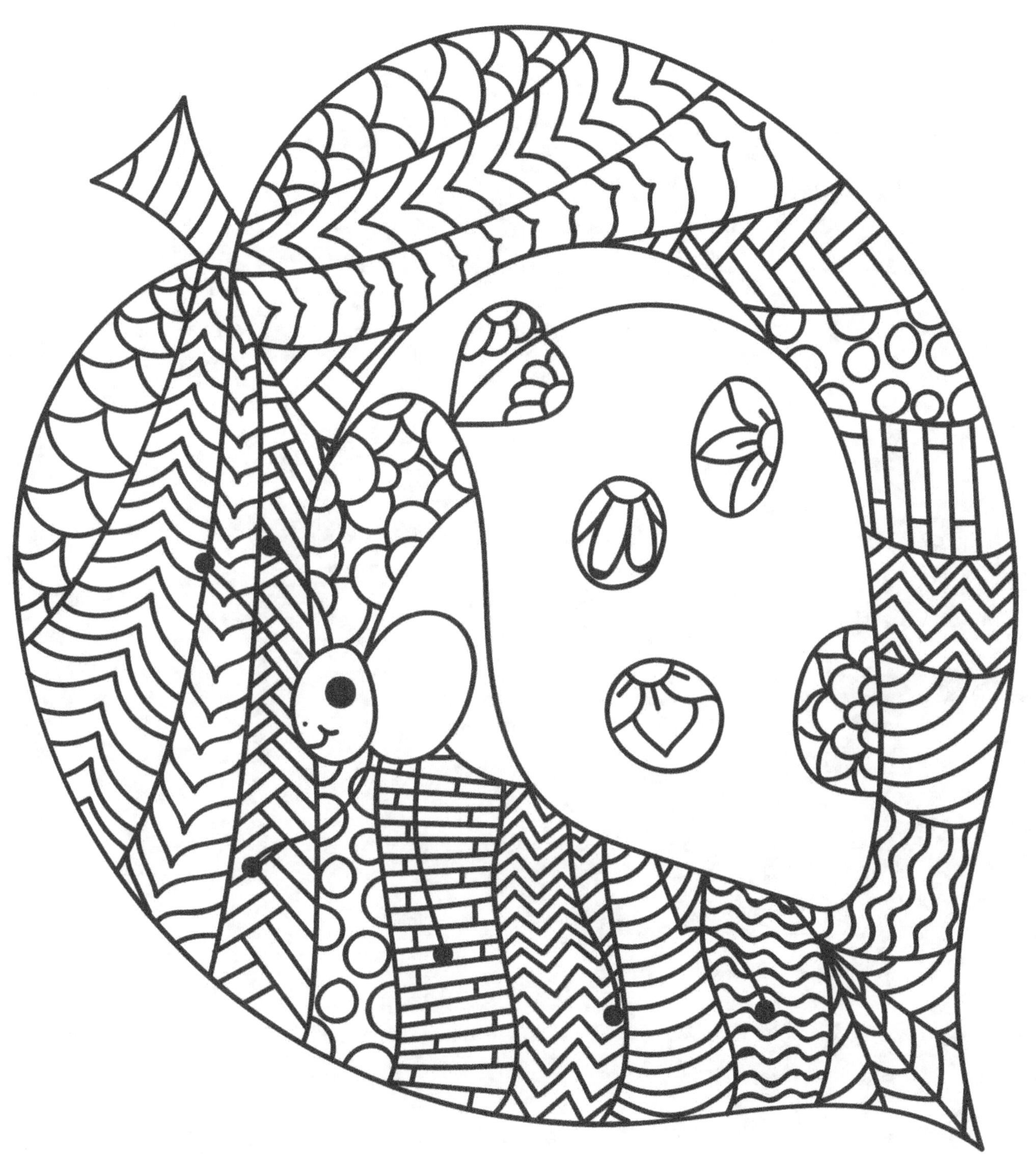

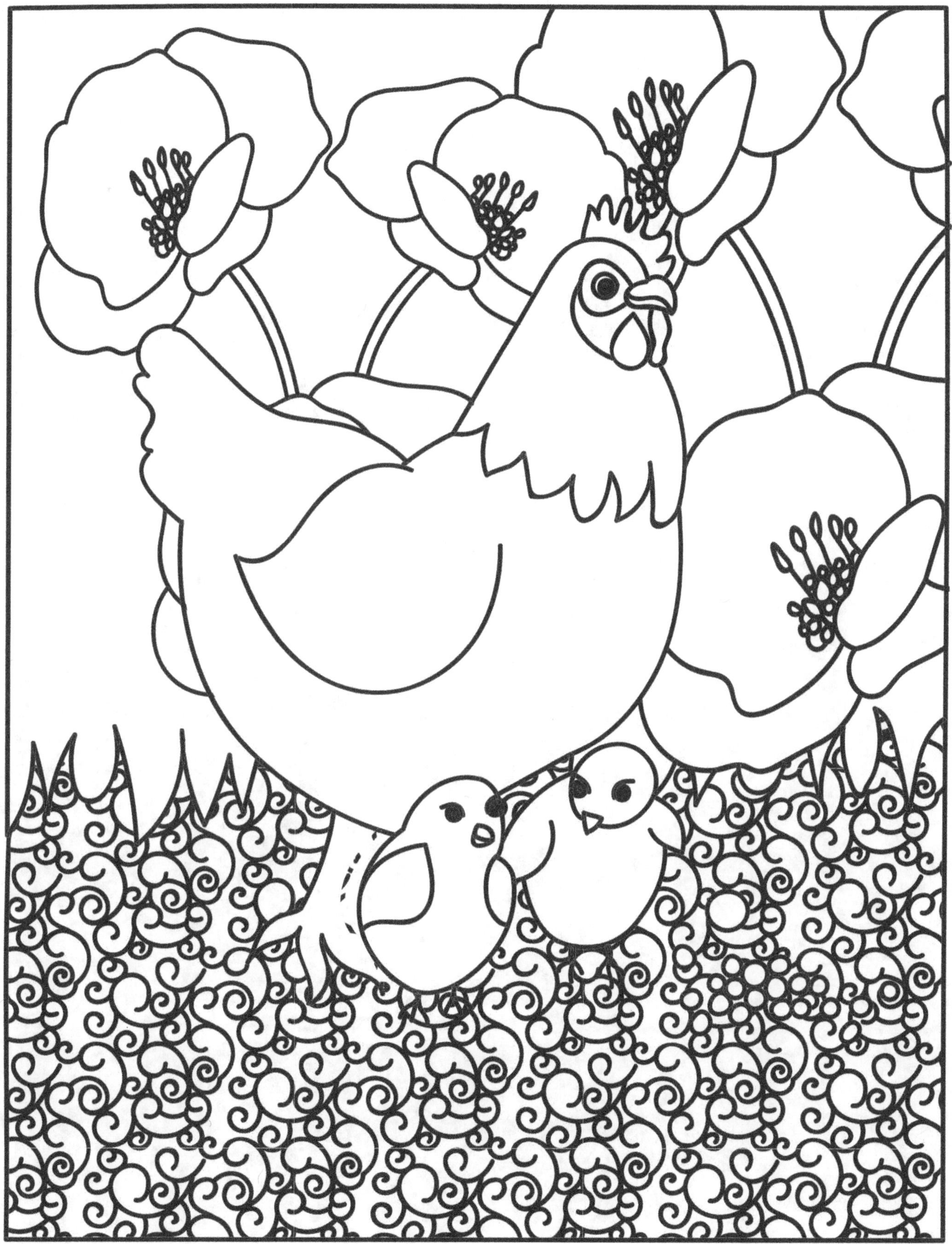

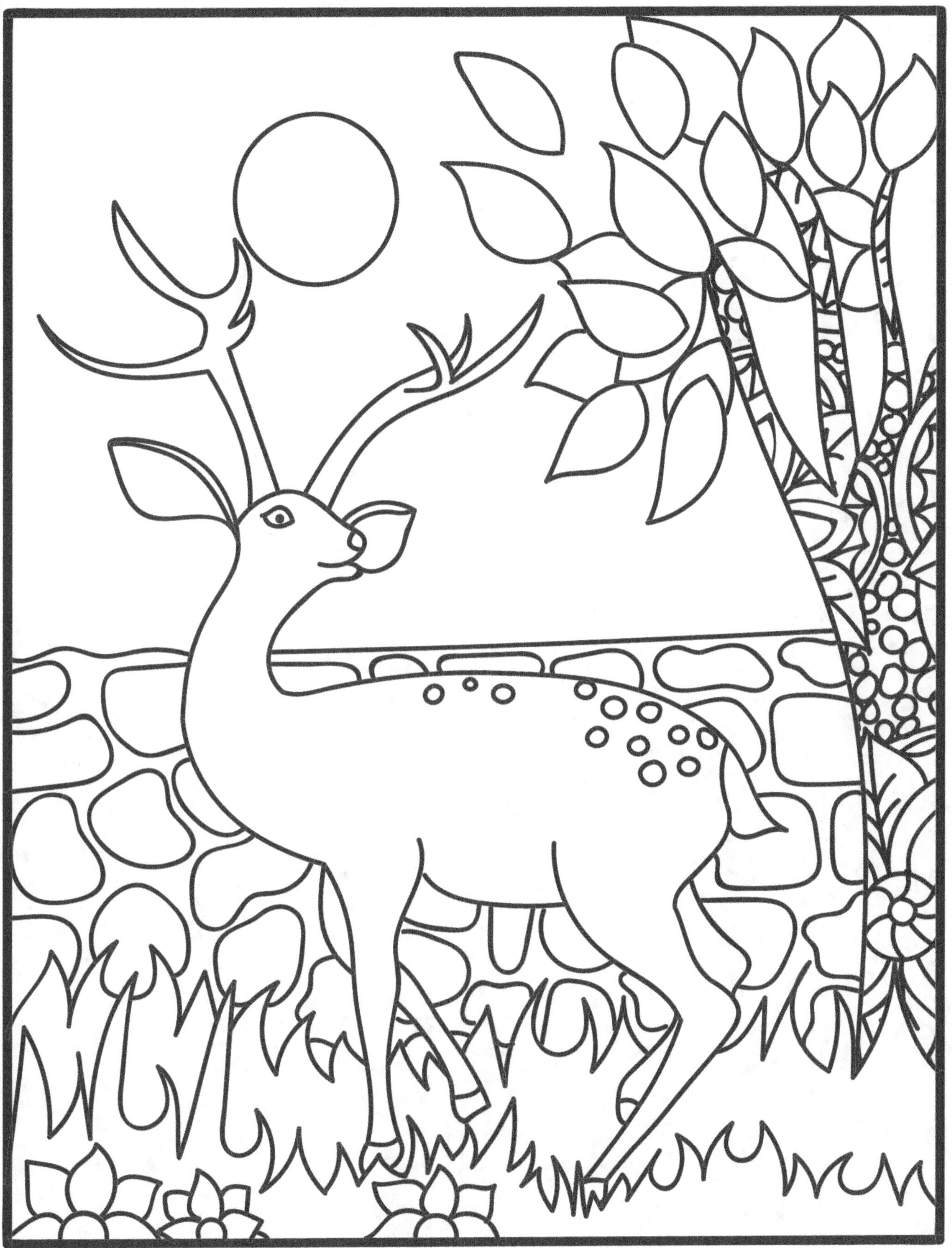

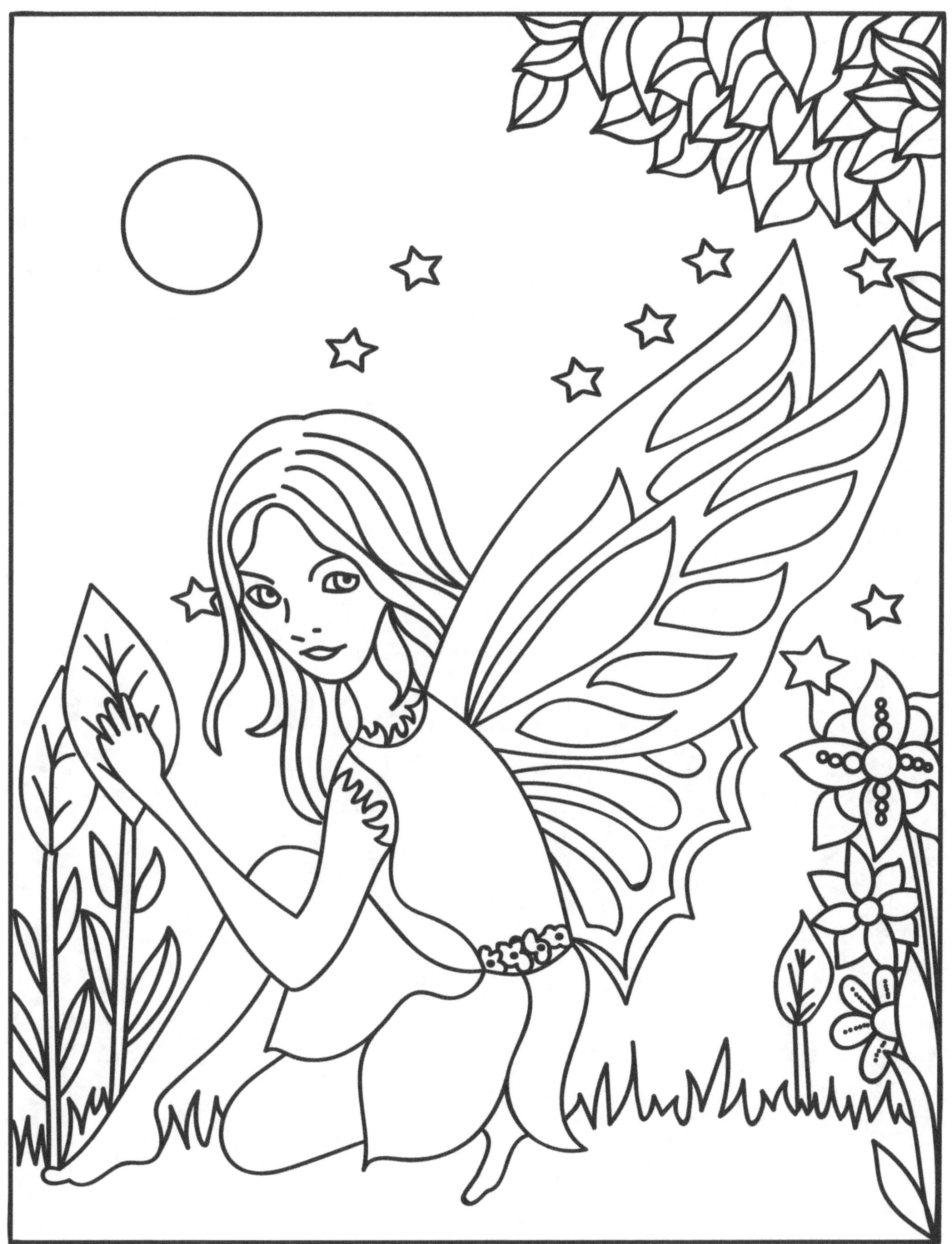

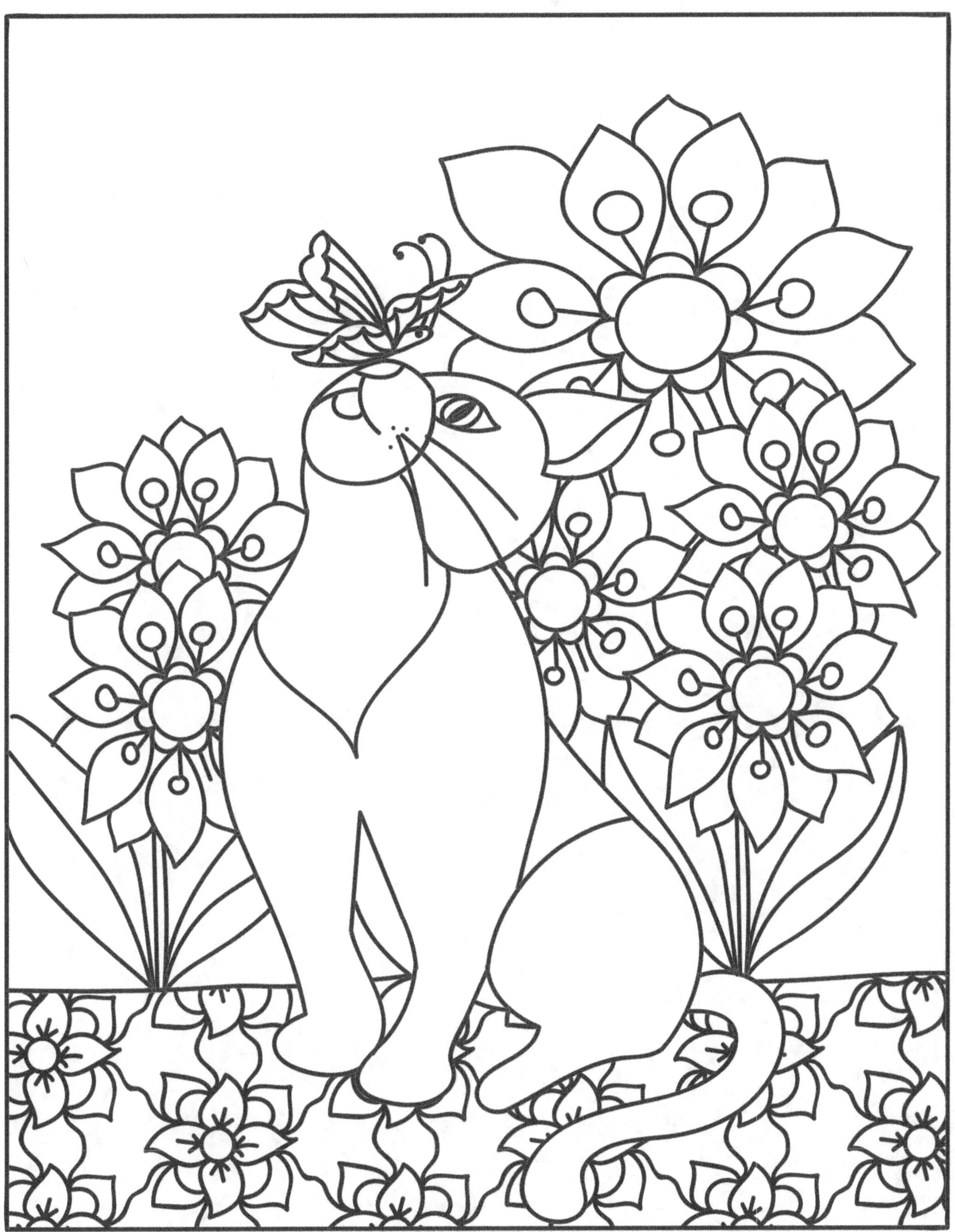

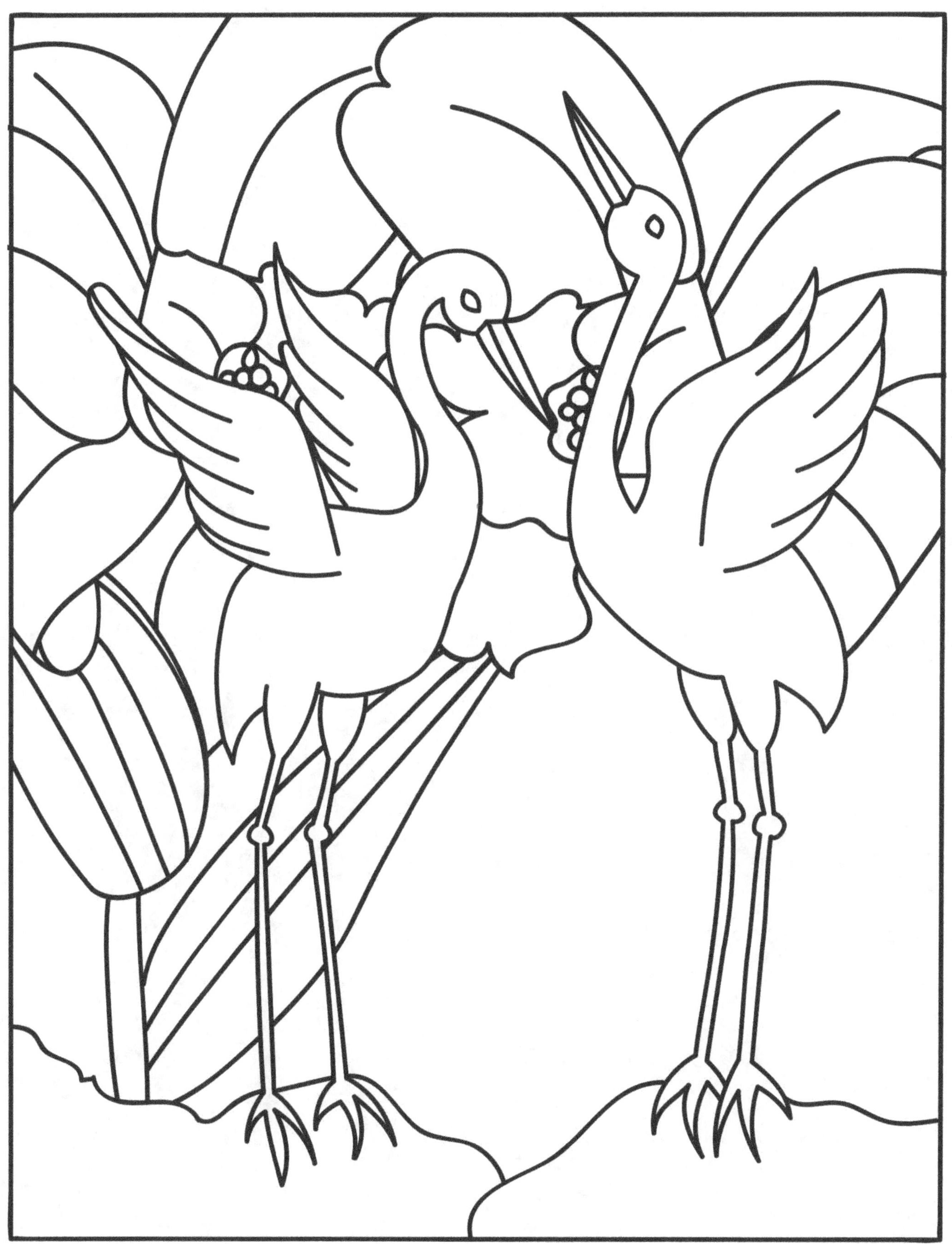

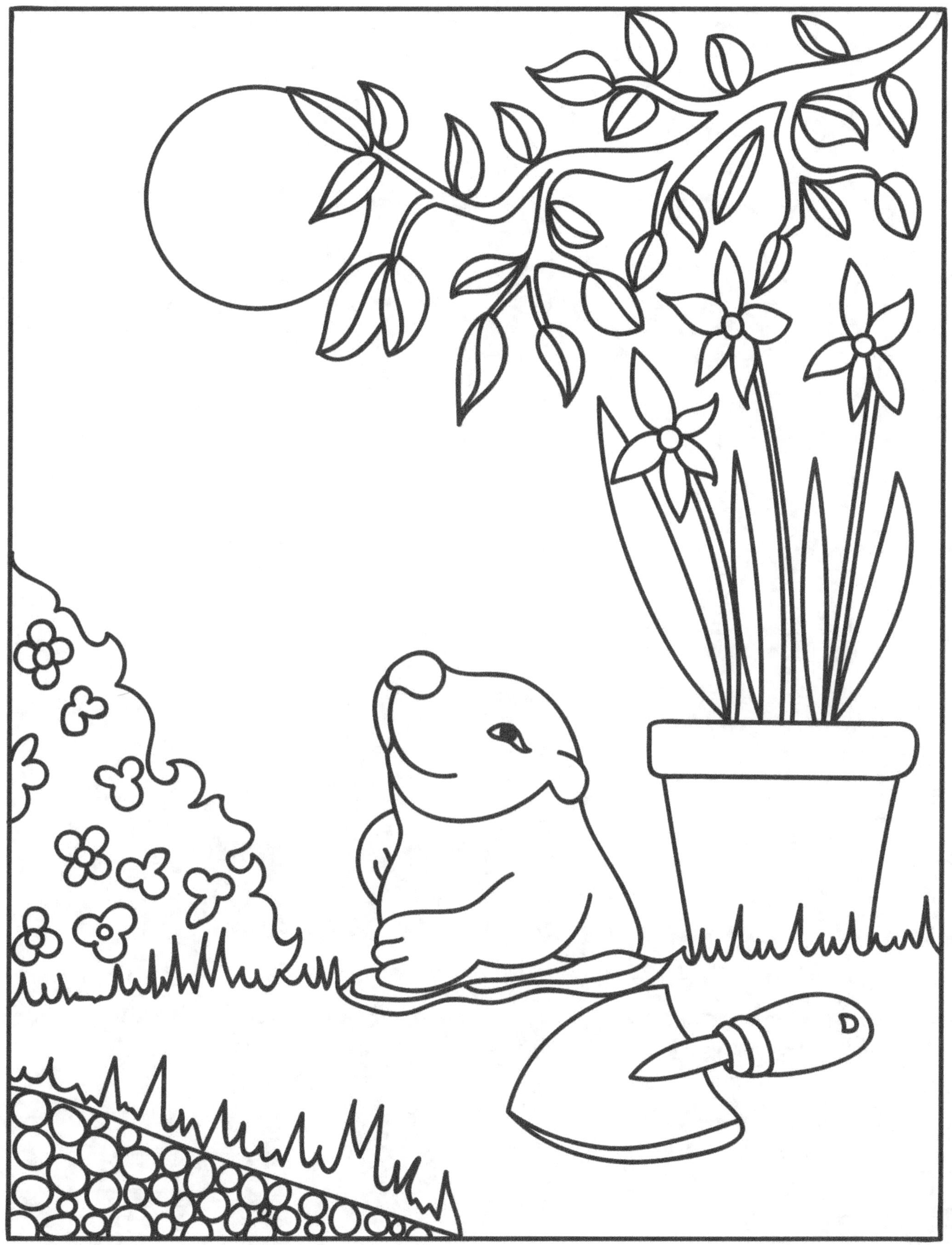

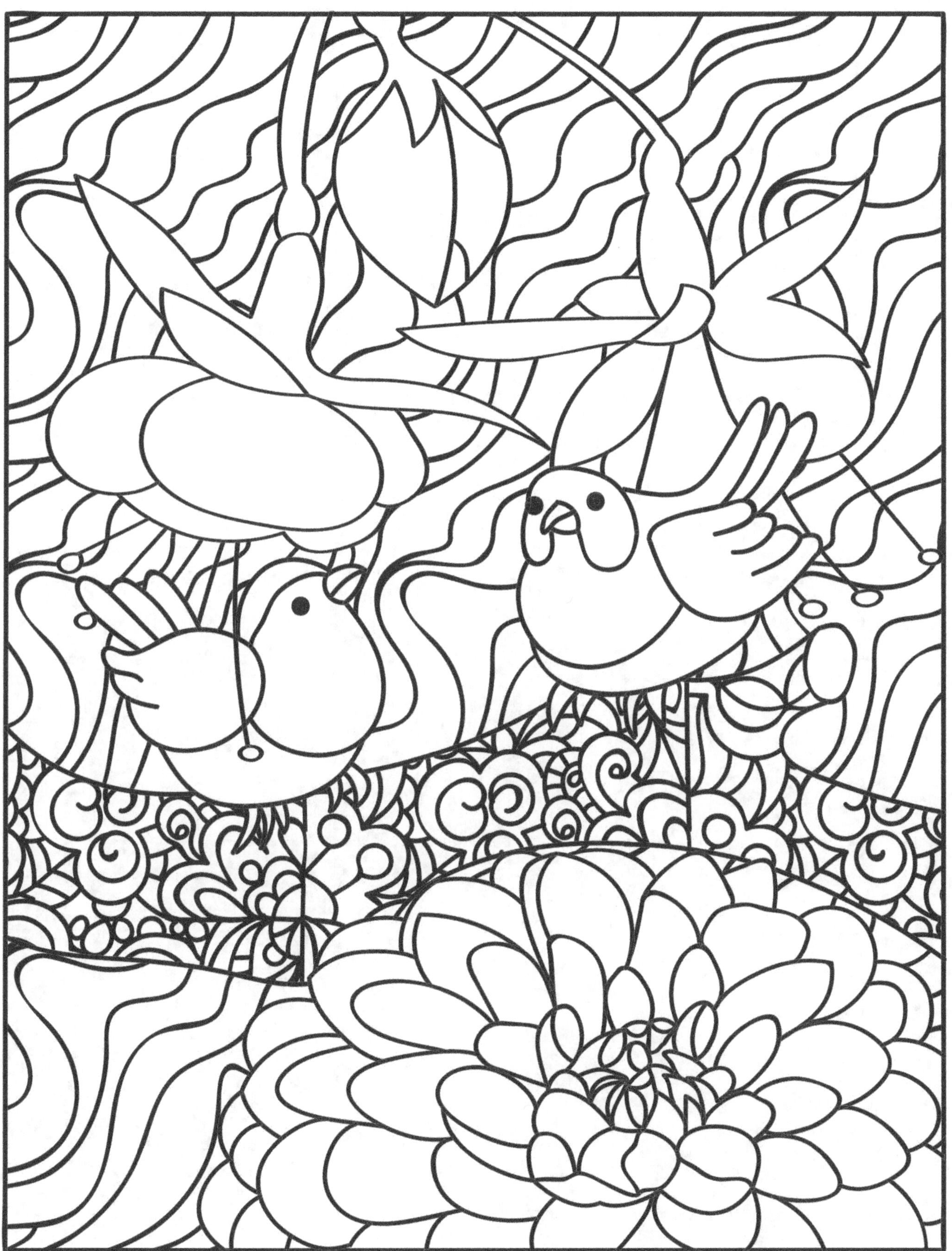

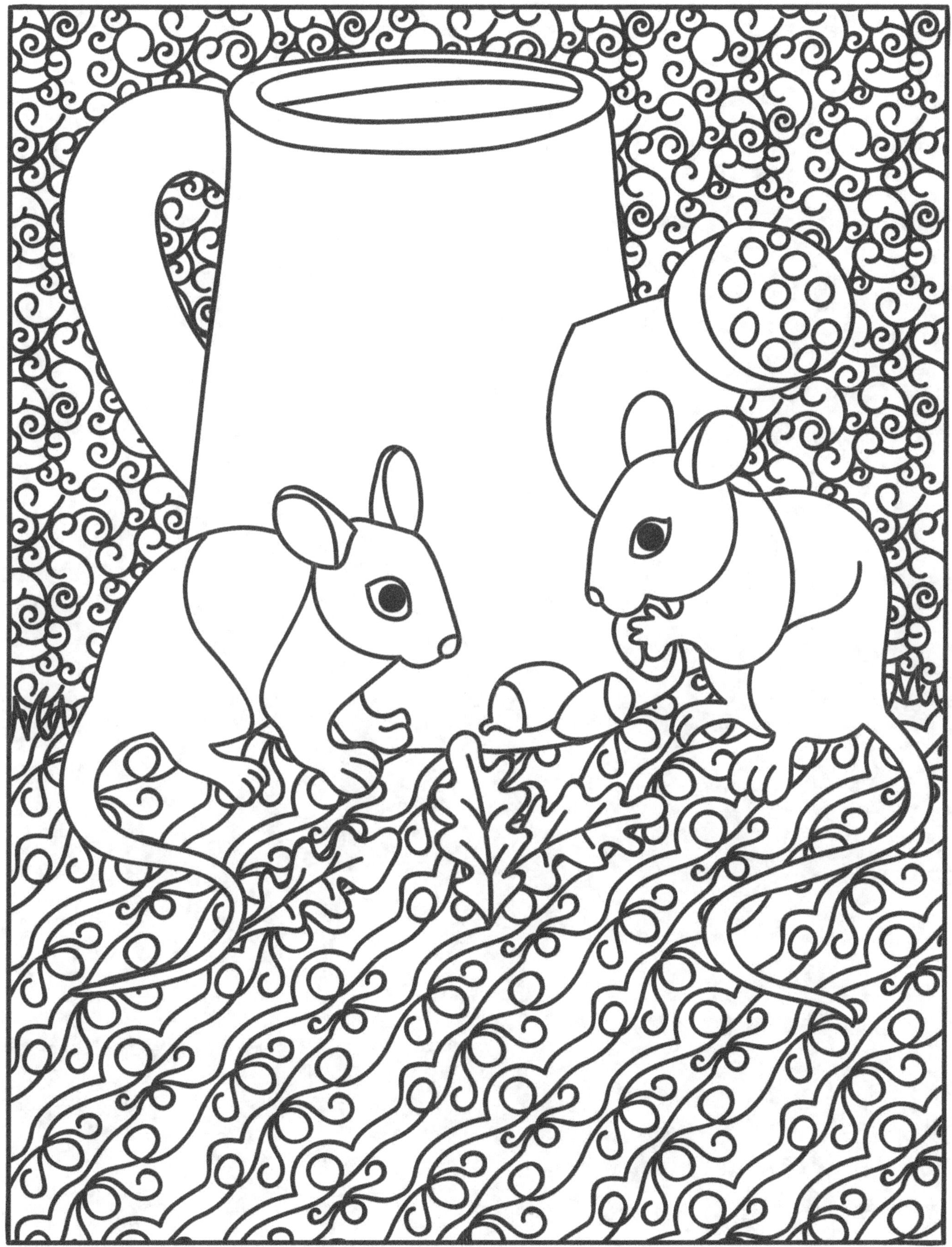

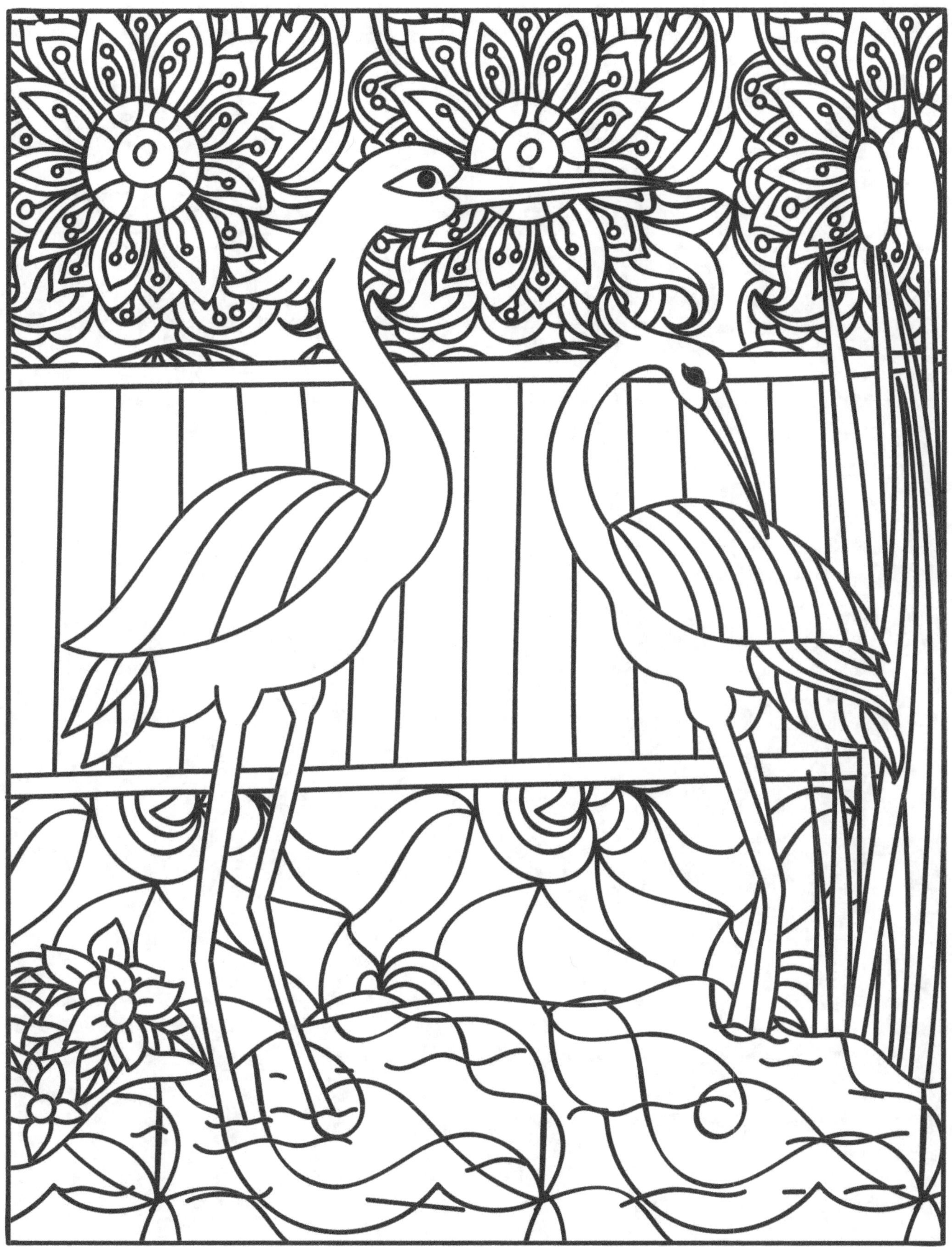

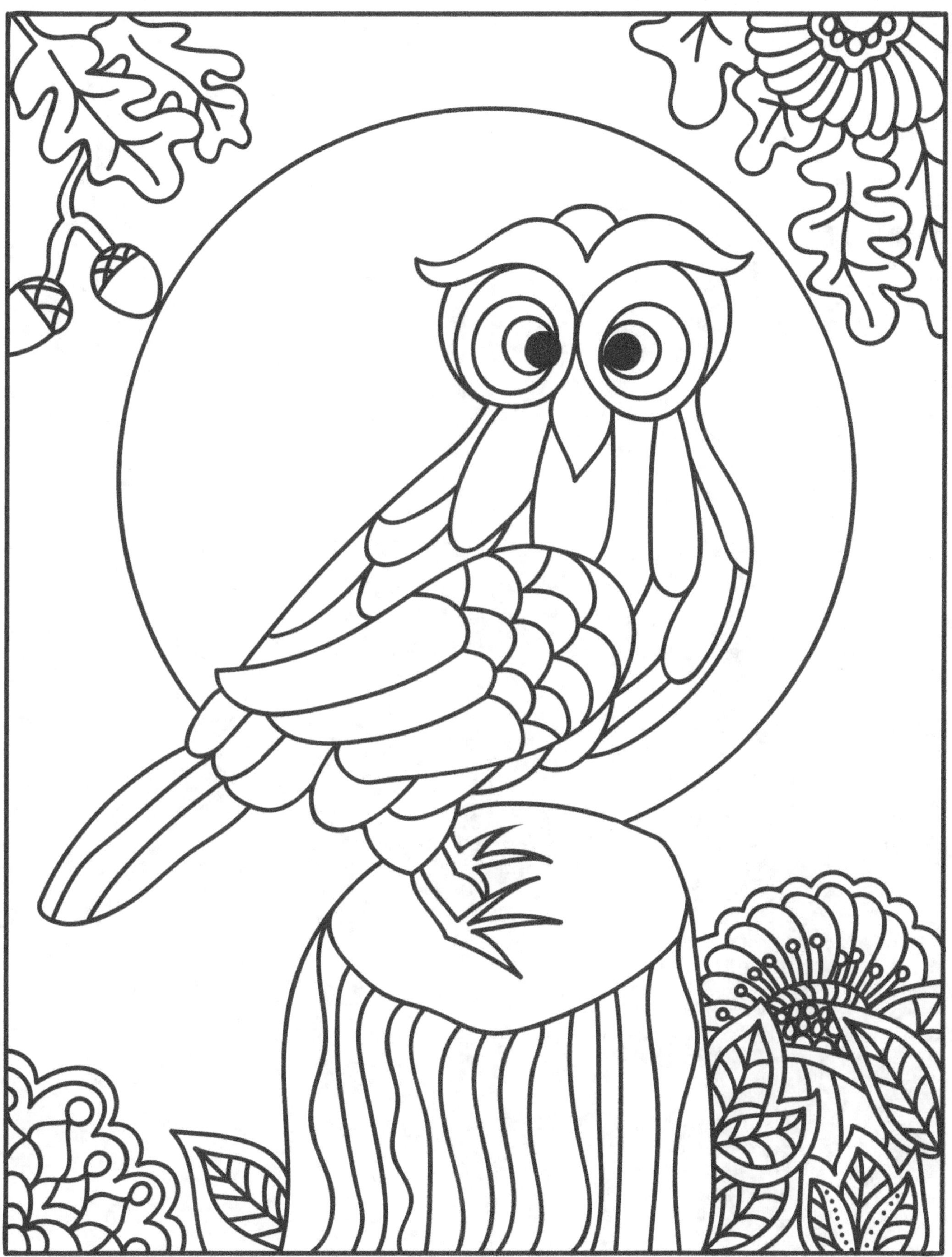

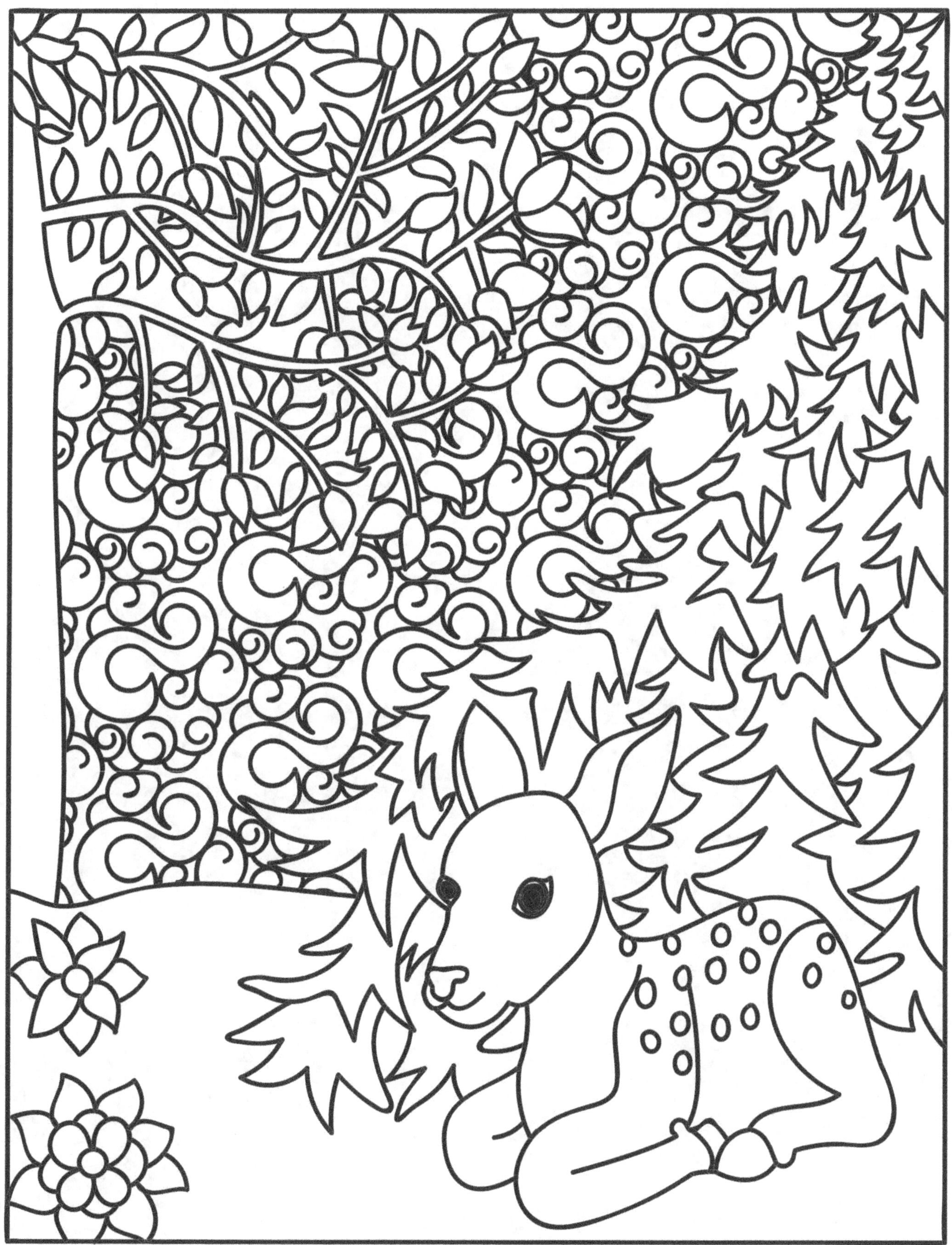

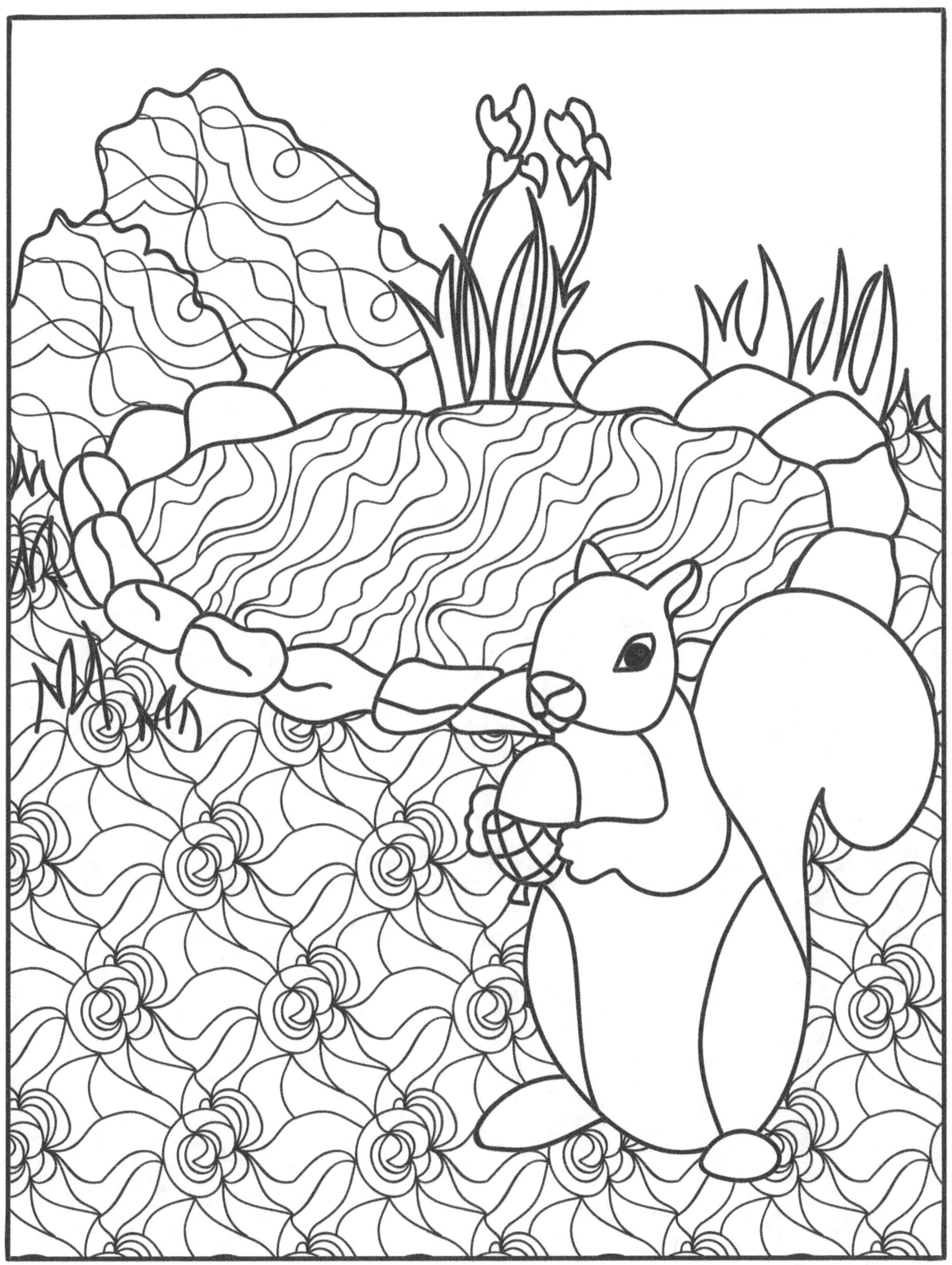

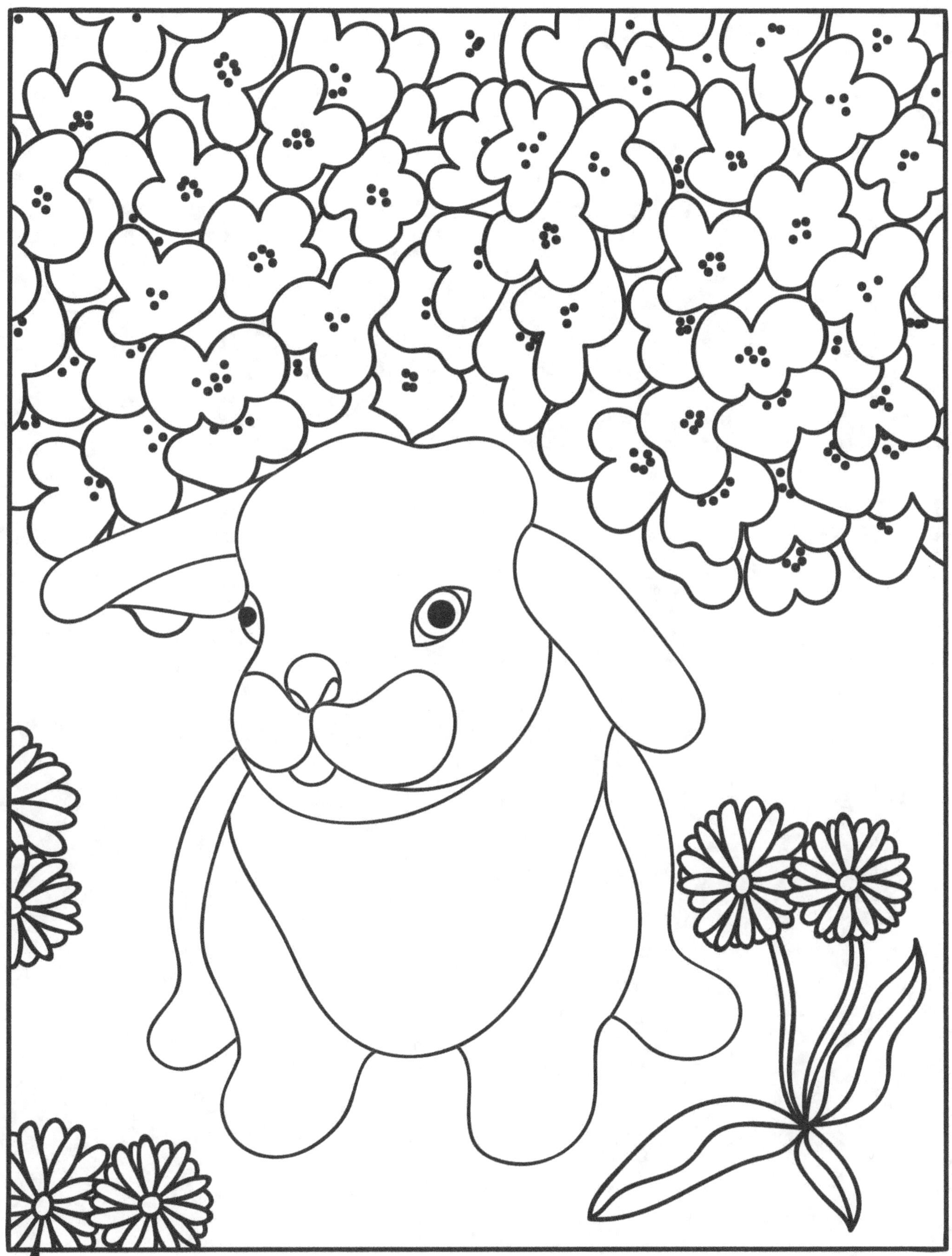

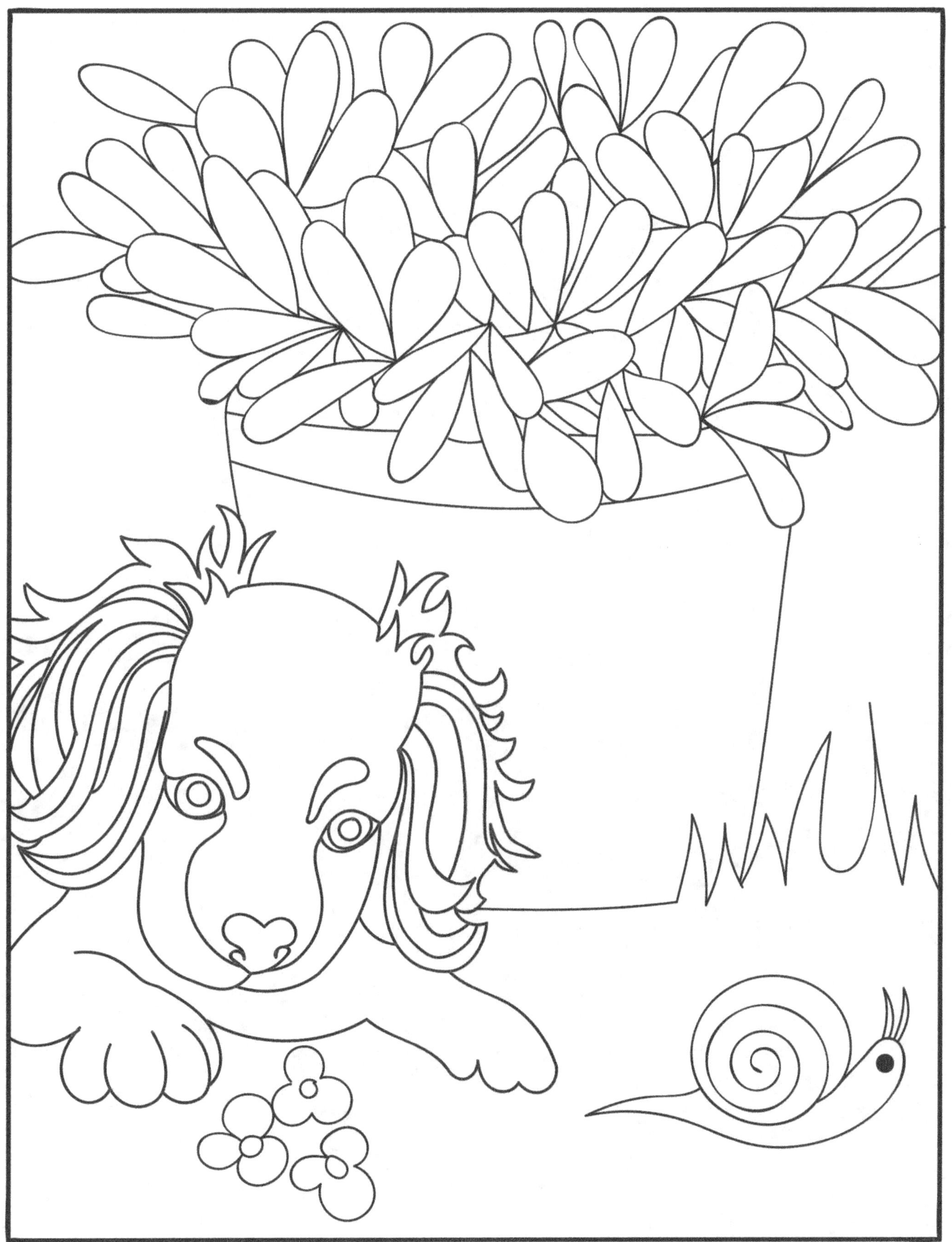

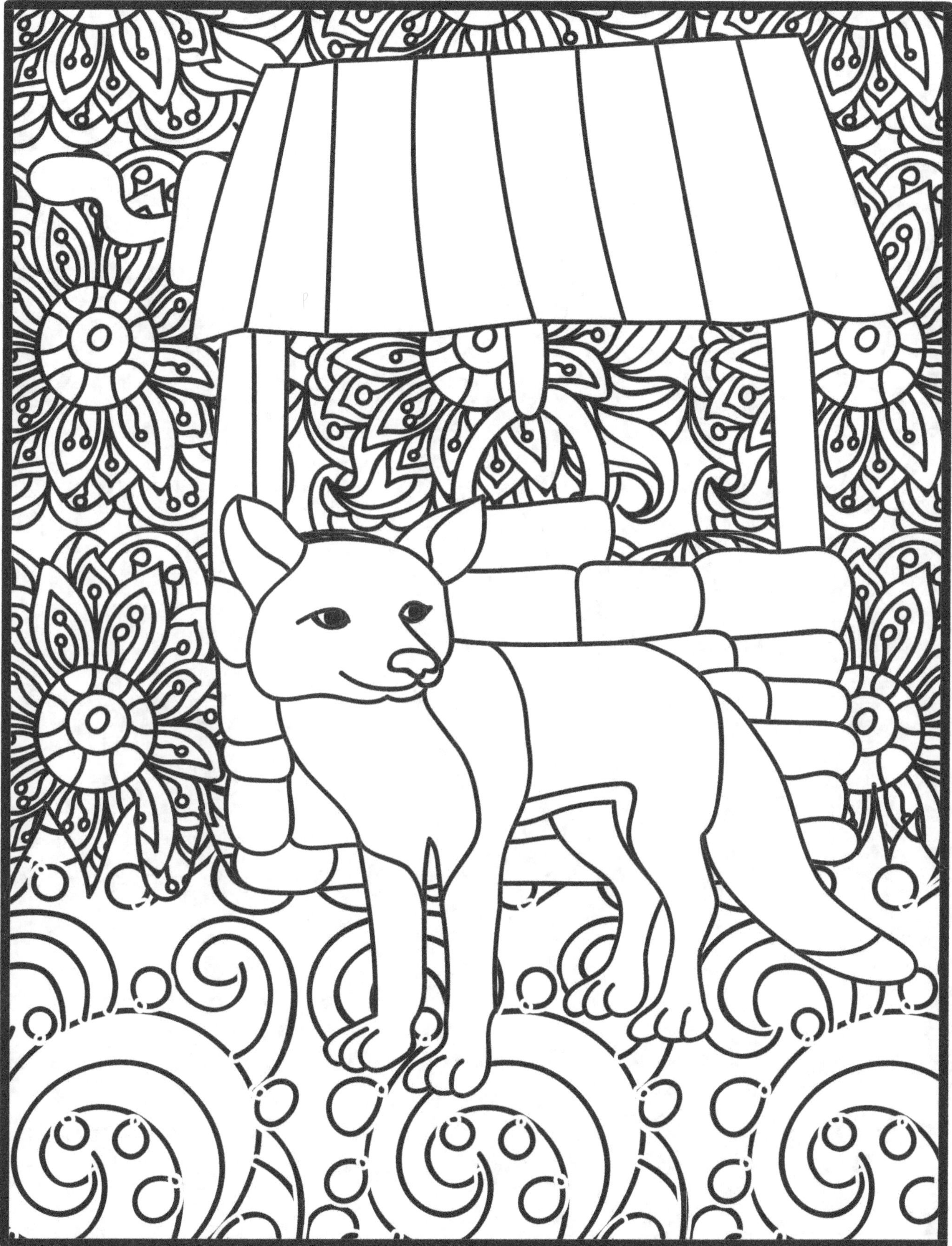

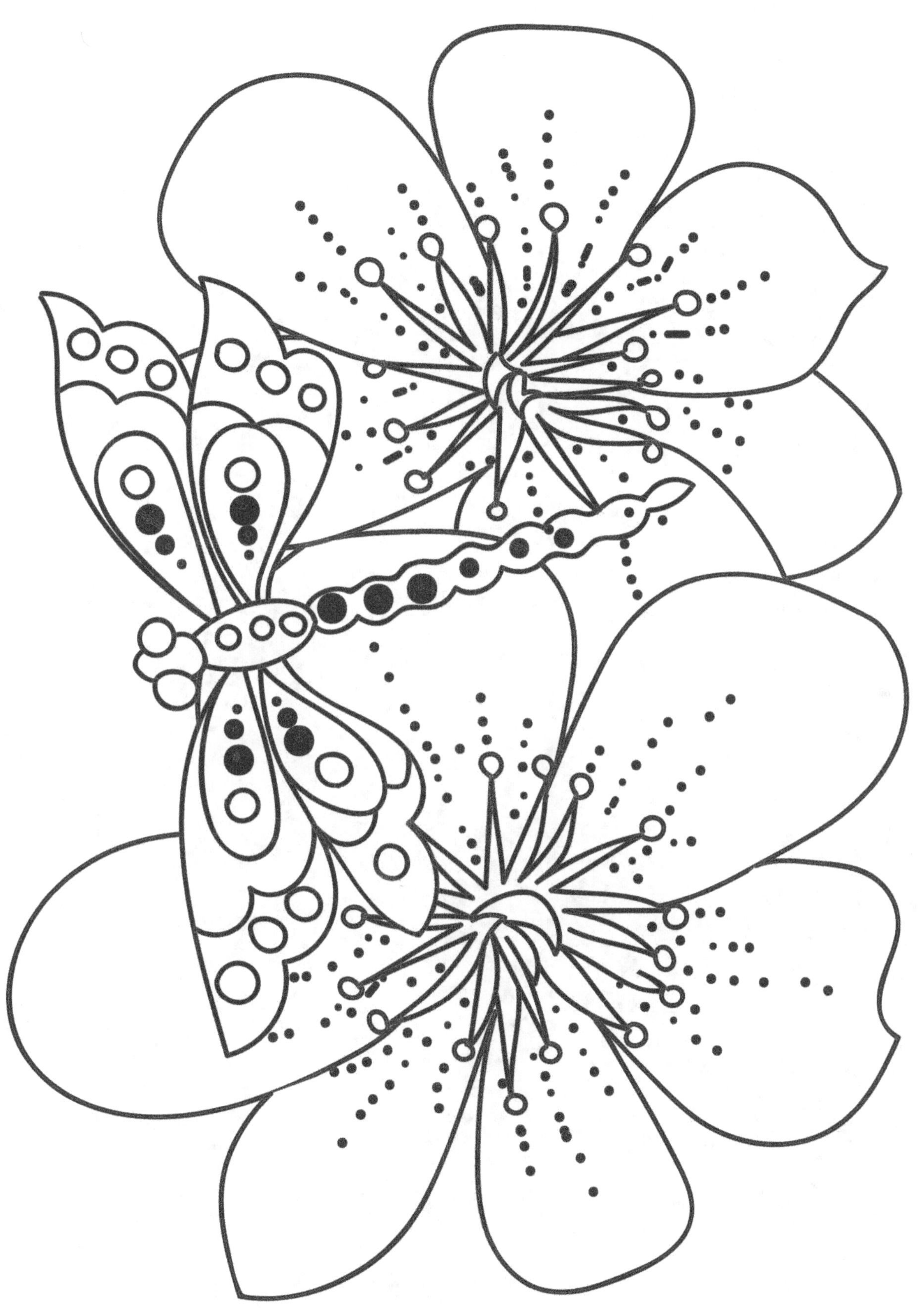

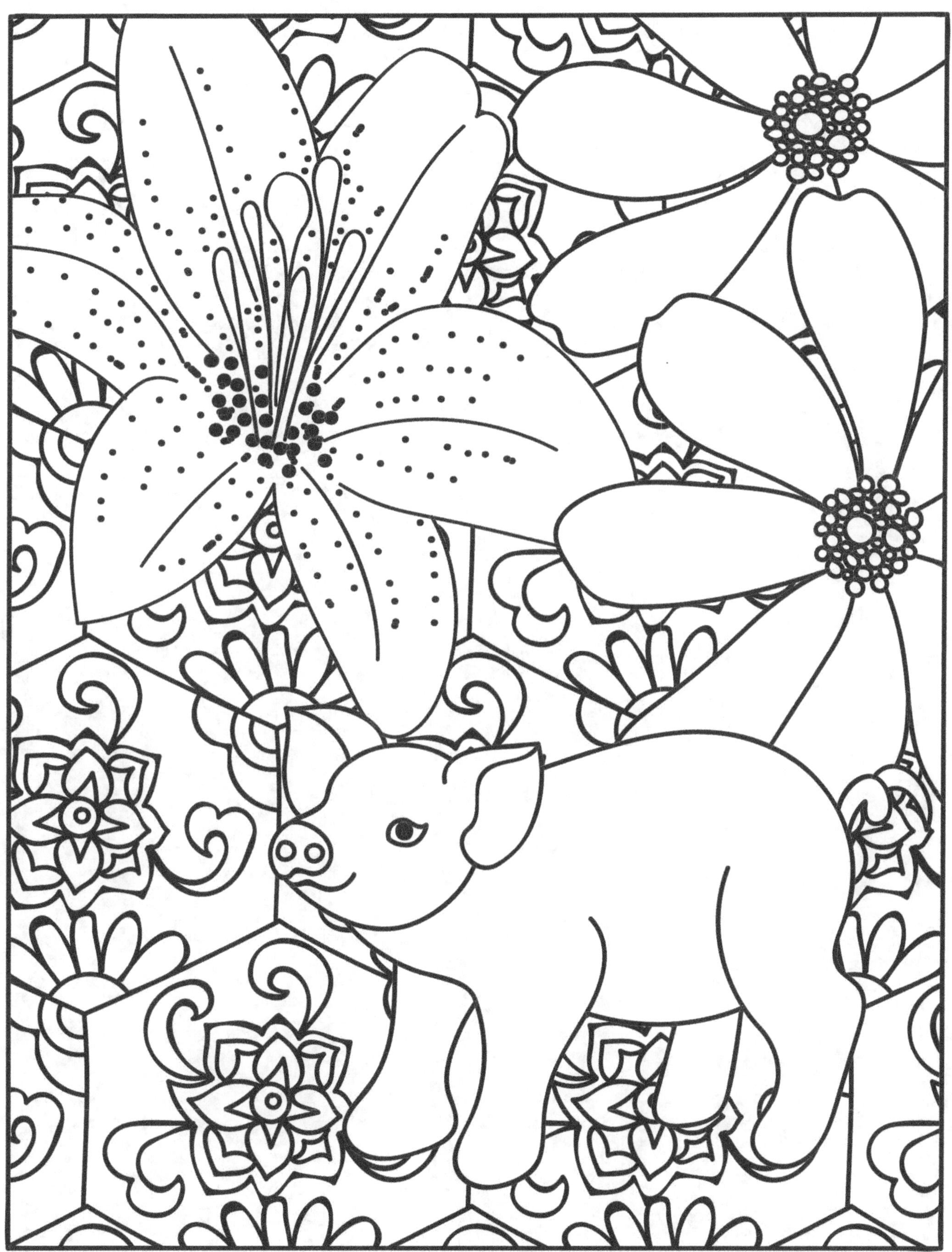

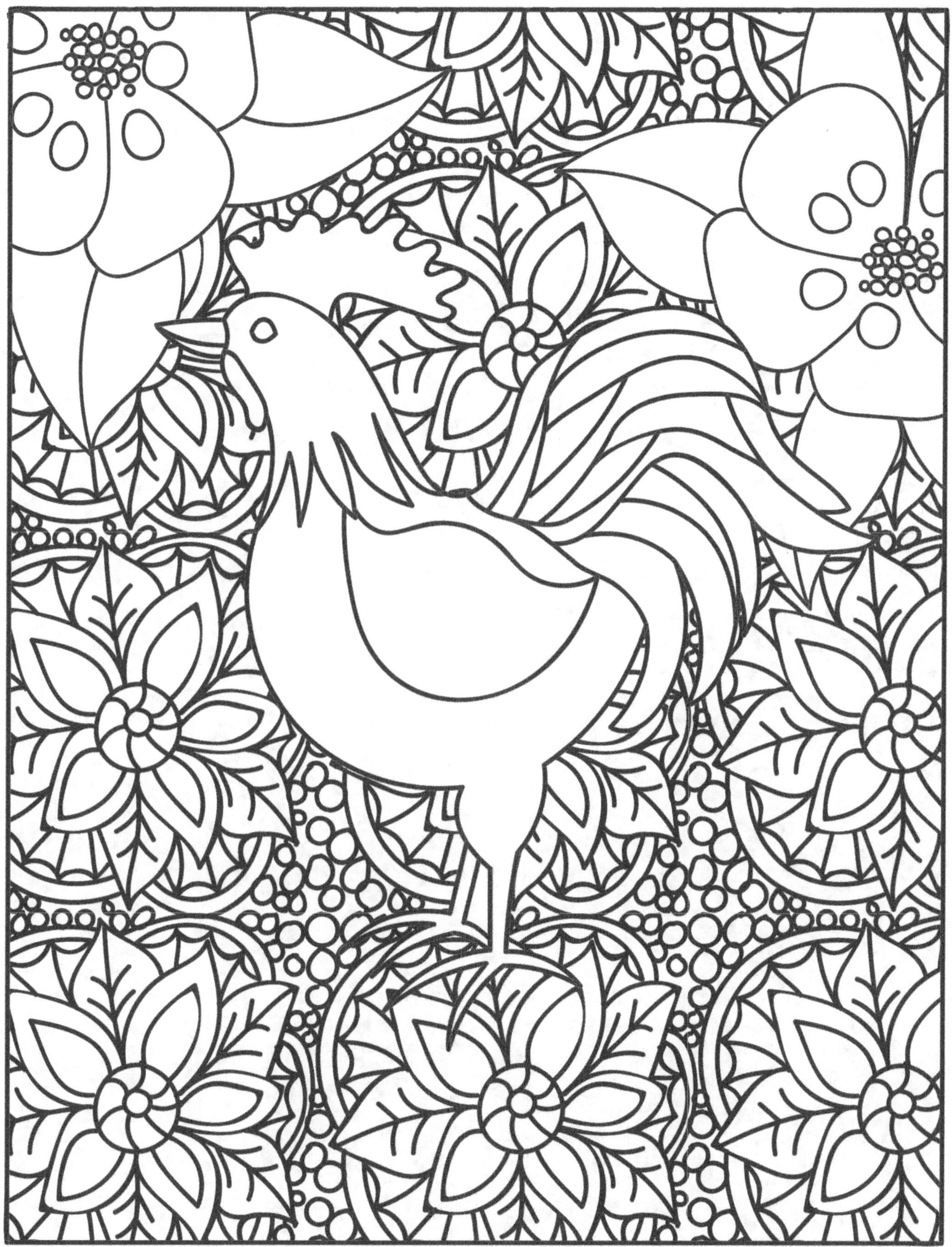

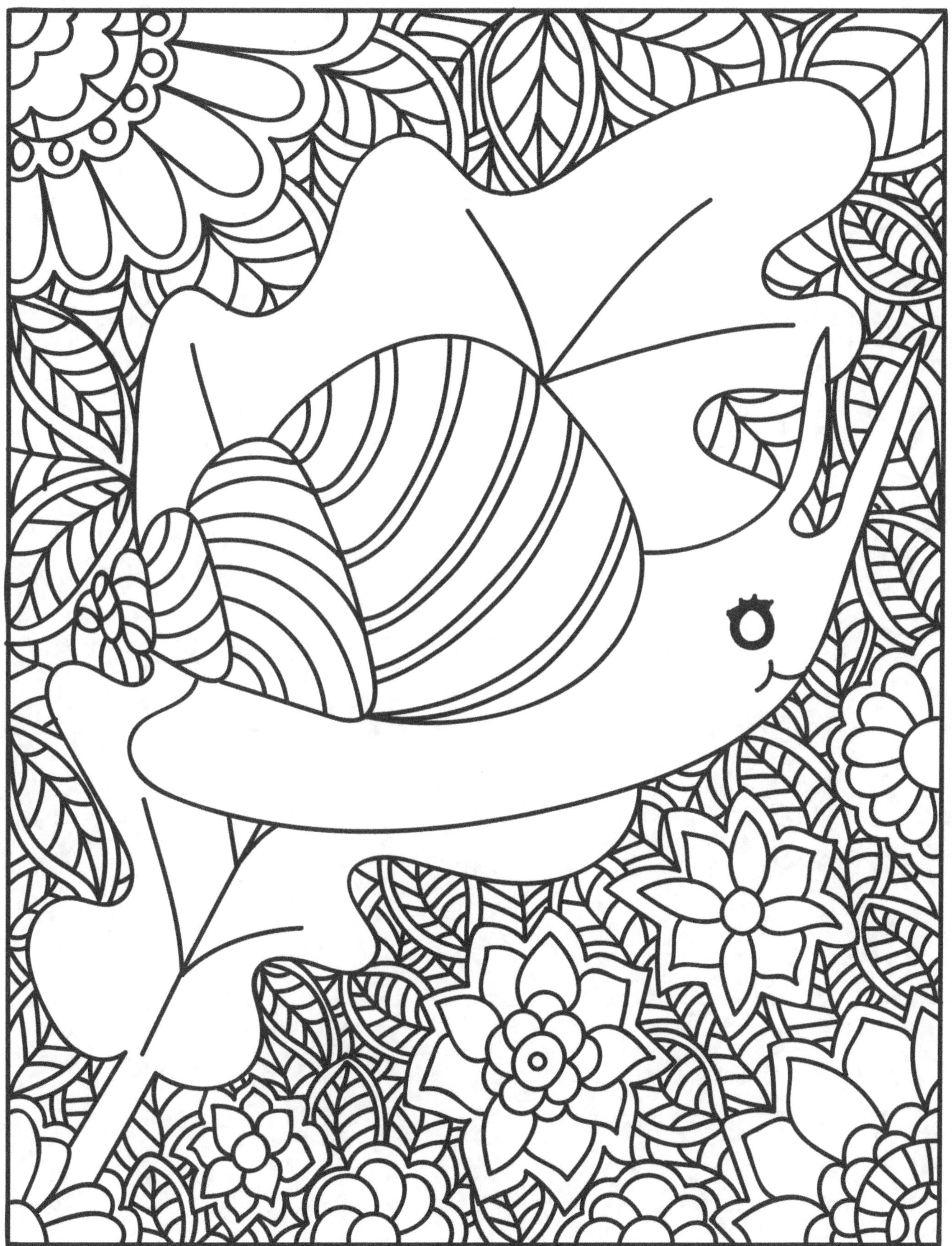

COLOR TEST PAGE

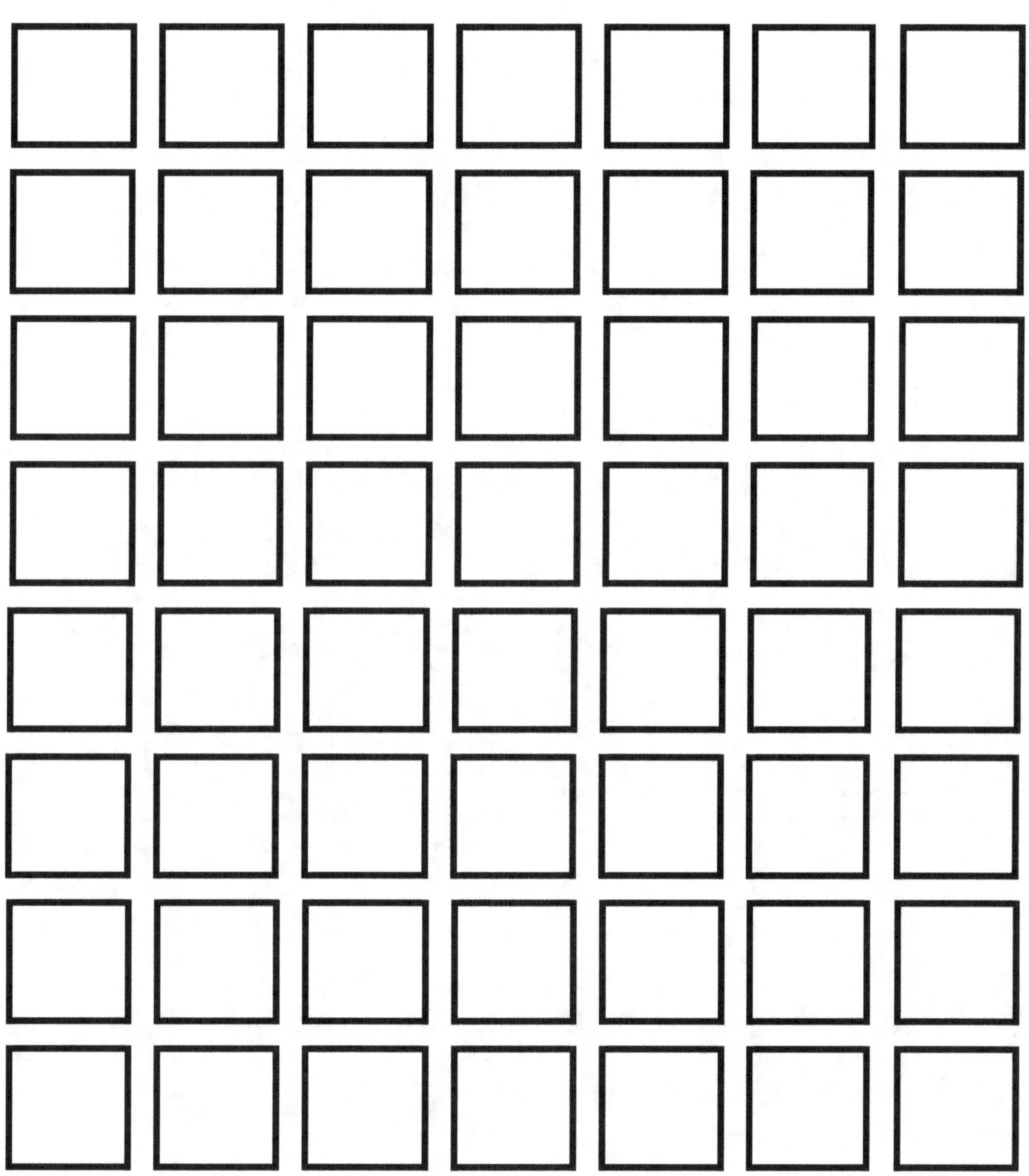

COLOR TEST PAGE

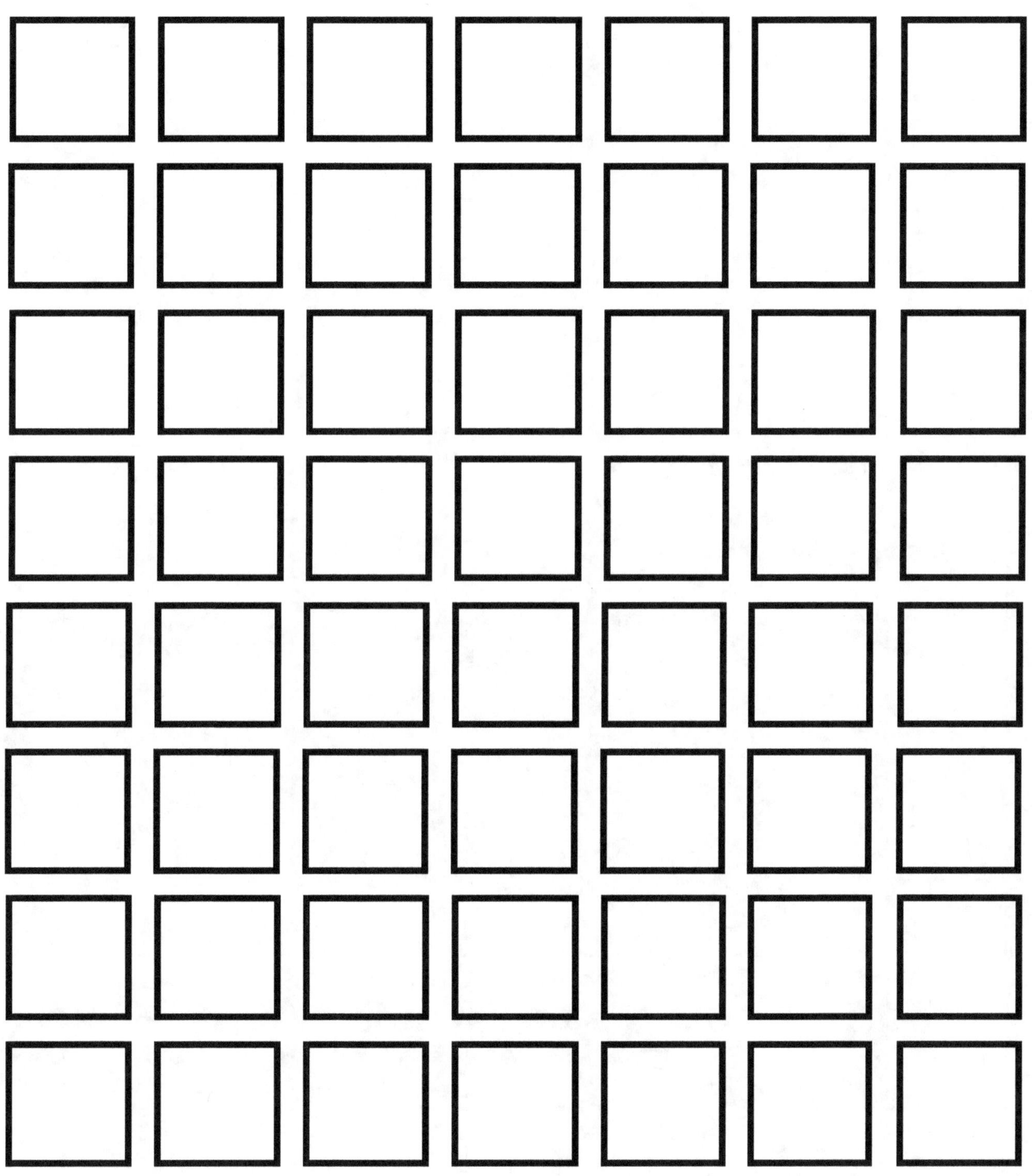